THE MEANING OF THE LITURGY

Philipp Harnoncourt
Angelus A. Häussling, o.s.b.
Klemens Richter
Richard Schaeffler
Philipp Schäfer
Clemens Thoma, s.v.d.

Angelus A. Häussling, o.s.b.
Editor

Linda M. Maloney
Translator

A Liturgical Press Book

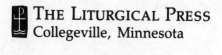

THE LITURGICAL PRESS
Collegeville, Minnesota

1   2   3   4   5   6   7   8

Library of Congress Cataloging-in-Publication Data

Vom Sinn der Liturgie. English.
   The Meaning of the Liturgy / Angelus A. Häussling, editor ; Angelus A. Häussling . . . [et al.] ; Linda M. Maloney, translator.
     p. cm.
   Translation of: Vom Sinn der Liturgie.
   Proceedings of a conference held Oct. 6-7, 1990, in Munich, Germany, arranged by the Catholic Academy of Bavaria.
   Includes bibliographical references.
   ISBN 0-8146-2273-9
   1. Catholic Church—Liturgy—Congresses. I. Häussling, Angelus Albert. II. Katholische Akademie in Bayern. III. Title.
BX1970.V64513 1994
264'.02—dc20
                                       94-7507
                                        CIP

Contents

Angelus A. Häussling, o.s.b.

Introduction:
The Meaning of the Liturgy

"The Meaning of the Liturgy" is neither an accurate nor an intriguing name for the conference arranged by the Catholic Academy of Bavaria in Munich on 6–7 October 1990. As a title for the book containing the papers presented there and making them available to a broader audience, it immediately reminds those familiar with the subject of the key essay with which Romano Guardini made his public debut in 1918, and which quickly made his a familiar name: *The Spirit of the Liturgy.* This slender book, which has been frequently reprinted since 1918, virtually without alteration (most recently in 1983 with an introduction by Hans Maier as number 1049 in the Herder Taschenbuch series), has reached a total of some 100,000 copies.

At the time of its first publication, it inaugurated the series *Ecclesia orans,* edited by Ildefons Herwegen (1874–1946), the abbot of Maria Laach. It stood like a signal flag at the beginning of the so-called liturgical movement in Germany. Its programmatic statement was that liturgy is not a passé ritual or a pious practice; it is life and it can give life. It is human life practiced in a form that draws individuals into the community of the Church and causes them to be who they truly are, precisely because it opens to them the objective realities of God in contrast to the subjective phenomena of the modern world. It was a stellar moment for Catholic Germany, occurring a few months before the First World War ended, bringing with it previously unthinkable and revolutionary changes in the political and intellectual world, sweeping away the familiar patterns of life and forcing a reorientation. At that moment Romano Guardini signaled, in words that were as beautiful as they were clear, that the liturgy was a heritage worth rediscovering, something that if properly understood— no, if properly celebrated—could and must renew the world of faith as it was then known.

The Catholic Academy of Bavaria certainly has a moral claim on Romano Guardini and the title of his book. It has assumed the rights to his literary work and sees in him, as one of the advisers at the time of its establishment, something like a spiritual founder; it honors his memory each year by the presentation of the highly respected Guardini Prize.

Does the academy also intend, by its choice of title, to say that Guardini's first book is still, or again, as contemporary as it was more than seventy years ago? Certainly that is not its intention. Let us leave aside for the moment the fact that, after the passage of three-quarters of a century, the spiritual landscape is truly no longer the same. What Guardini and his supporter Herwegen scarcely dared to dream has in the meantime become reality: an ecumenical council of the Roman Catholic Church adopted the essential ideas of the "liturgical movement" as its own. Still more: it did something those active at the time had not even thought of, by accomplishing a renewal of the form of the liturgy to make it for the Church throughout the world what, according to the profound conviction of the promoters of the liturgical movement, it was meant to be: the home of faith, where God and the human being, in the unity of the celebration, arrive at the goal of the work of salvation. Guardini and Herwegen were interested in the renewal of the Christian religious mentality through the "spirit of the liturgy."

In view of the pluralism of the modern world, and even of the religious mentality, they thought that the liturgy should be the collecting point where faith, the worship of God, and the Church as community would again be united and where Christians could achieve the personal integrity that would be absolutely necessary for them in meeting the demands of a new era. "In the spirit of the liturgy" means renewal drawn from that which liturgy is in itself. (For that reason, Herwegen did not like to hear talk of a "liturgical movement," and preferred to speak of "liturgical renewal.") That the liturgy would have to change the Church itself in order to fulfill the task they had found for it appeared to the minds of these Christians, pastors, and theologians, if at all, as a very distant possibility. The precious culture of the West was still taken too much for granted, and their relationship to it was still too unruffled; their trust in the wealth of its tradition was too secure, and their distance from the catastrophes of European history was too small for them to recognize how deep the rifts really went. (At that moment, the collapse of public morality in the Third Reich was still unimaginable.) They simply could not see that the liturgy, indisputably part of that culture and even in some sense its true center, since its purpose was the obligatory and unceasing worship of God, was insufficient in the form it then possessed.

If now, a quarter-century after the Second Vatican Council's Constitution on the Liturgy (*Sacrosanctum concilium*), a conference of the academy deals with "the meaning of the liturgy," it might seem at first glance as if this were a sign that the "liturgical movement" has, in fact, not achieved its purpose: for should not the "meaning of the liturgy" have been obvious for a long time now? But that would be jumping to conclusions. There was a concrete reason for the meeting. It was meant to be an anniversary celebration which would present to an interested public matters that, in the first days of the meeting, would be discussed in the closed circle of those immediately concerned. Its purpose was to commemorate the half-century since the German Bishops' Conference (at that time still called the "Fulda Bishops' Conference," but sometimes also including the bishops of Austria) appointed a "liturgical commission" consisting of representatives drawn from the "liturgical movement" and from experts in liturgiology. The recollection of that moment immediately showed how providential the creation of that group had been and how, unexpectedly, it had exercised influence beyond Germany and in the Church all over the world. The Second Vatican Council would not have been able to discuss and pass the Constitution on the Liturgy as its very first document—and in the process discover its own method of working—had the members of this group not previously named and deliberated the existing problems, made suggestions and circulated them, weathered crises with wisdom and decisiveness, sought international contacts and thereby practiced catholicity, and throughout all this dealt with "the meaning of the liturgy." But here again it was evident that these beginnings were already history. The present poses new questions, even questions of principle, and most prominently the question of the meaning of liturgy itself. Anyone who deals honestly with the liturgy at this point, ten years before the beginning of the third millennium of the Church's history, must grapple with this question.

Of course, the conference did not claim to treat, even remotely, the entire breadth of the question of "the meaning of the liturgy." It did what such meetings are meant to do: it incited people to reflect, and even to rethink. For this purpose it was sufficient that certain aspects of the question should be illuminated. This was the only aim of the speakers in giving their papers and in responding to participants' questions in the discussions that followed. Without regard for the sequence of the conference in itself or in this publication series, we intend to present in this book a systematic arrangement (not obligatory, but perhaps appropriate) of the individual themes in order to help our readers to pose the question of "the meaning of the liturgy" for themselves today, so that they may think along with us and ultimately may answer the question through their intelligent participation in the liturgy.

Klemens Richter summarizes what we may call the major purpose of liturgical renewal. Its concern was not with liturgy as such, as if to make it nobler and more beautiful, and its execution more meaningful, would suffice. There had already been enough effort in that direction, at least in our part of the world, and for a long time past the scandalous situations that existed at the beginning of the Reformation had been eliminated. The purpose of liturgical renewal was the renewal of the Church itself, recognizing that the celebration of the liturgy is the heart of the Church. When the Council, respecting the concrete situation before it, prescribed a reform of the liturgy, it too intended nothing less than a renewal of the Church itself. The opening sentences of the conciliar Constitution on the Liturgy, in fact, state this with all the clarity that could be desired.

Richter then immediately introduces the slogan that was programmatically stated in 1918, the year of Guardini's *The Spirit of the Liturgy,* in the very next publication in the series *Ecclesia orans:* "The Lord's Memorial in the Ancient Christian Liturgy." The author was Odo Casel, a Benedictine of Maria Laach, and the title of his book was also a summary of his wide-ranging theological life's work. But what, in the book's title, was stated as historical fact has been recognized and acknowledged in the meantime (not without the contribution of the theologian Casel, himself) as the indispensable characteristic of the liturgy itself: it is a memorial. In it, remembering, the Church and the Christians come in contact with the Lord's work of salvation, a contact that is saving because it is sacramentally and ontically relevant. Only in this way does the Church remain the community of those who believe in Christ, are touched by his word, and celebrate his sacraments. When liturgy is the subject, what is at issue is the Church as a whole, not some trivial matter within the Church. Reform of the liturgy is reform of the Church, and this reform will not cease as long as the Church continues to exist. No Council can know what concrete steps this reform will have to dare, after the lapse of twenty-five years, in order to remain true to its major and only theme: the Church of the Lord that is worthy of belief and that worships God with Christ in the unity of the Spirit.

The essay by Philipp Schäfer also peers, as it were, into the interior of the Church. Here the theme is the very event that is remembered in the Church's memorial, namely, the death and resurrection of the Lord, and the place where it occurs most intensively, namely, the Eucharistic celebration. He is able to show that the theology of the last several decades has learned new ways of dealing with the idea of "memorial," and that the Church's teaching office has adopted the liturgical movement's deepening of our understanding of the sacraments and taught it to the Church.

Clemens Thoma brings a new accent, also with respect to what the theologians of the liturgical renewal perceived and expressed. He points out that the Jews, the first chosen people of God, acknowledged the salvation received from their God in no other way than by "memorial" and celebrated it that way in its songs and festivals. Of course, as far back as the record extends, the liturgy has always employed the noble songs of the Jewish Scriptures in celebrating the Lord's memorial. But we in the Church have become too accustomed to regarding, even cheapening the ancient prophecies as promises, preliminary annunciations that have been fulfilled in the Church and therefore made redundant. Not least are the unimaginably horrible events symbolized by the name of Auschwitz that have helped us to learn that the covenant with Israel was never abrogated and that therefore Israel's worship is valid in God's sight; also that we Christians misread our own reality when we think we need only surpass what once was merely temporary. That is not the reality. There is but a single people of God, because it is united by a single memory: the memory of God's saving deeds. The saving actions of Jesus the Christ are not to be thought of as different from YHWH's saving actions on behalf of Abraham and his people. This insight, which has by no means been accepted in its full implications and in sufficient breadth, is also one of the very few new discoveries that can be pointed out in the theology of the last several decades.

In contrast, the remaining essays are less concerned with the Church itself and more with those ones who are to become Church and who are nowadays the major concern of everyone who cares for humanity and its life: the people themselves. How do they live, what are their opportunities to celebrate the indispensable, saving memorial in such a way that they can make it their own?

As Philipp Harnoncourt asserts, the praise of God is a fundamental form of human existence. The fact that human beings are made for dialogue, that they regularly long for the exuberance of festal celebration, that their language, when it is joyful, becomes poetry and music: all this shows that where the work of liturgy is absent, where it fails or is denied, human nature is not fulfilled. Liturgy cannot cease if human beings want to remain themselves.

Another aspect of human nature, certainly, is the impulse to ask questions. And the question of modern people when they hear about the "memorial" of something past must be:

how can the past be remembered in such a way that it becomes my concern, here and now? Only when this question and others like it are taken seriously can believable liturgy be celebrated. Angelus A. Häußling, a Benedictine of Maria Laach, the abbey that has already been mentioned twice, desires to take this question seriously and to draw attention to the stylistic means by which the Christians of the post-apostolic generation demonstrated that the Lord's saving deeds, which they remembered in faith and celebration, were their own possession, their own present life.

It is clear that, in a narrow sense of the word, these means were not typically "Christian." They are elementally human, even appropriate to times and regions where atheists are the ordinary citizens and believers an anomaly. When liturgy is our topic, we can no longer speak so unquestioningly of God, and almost nothing but God, as was possible in the initial phases of the liturgical renewal. "Our concern is for the human being"—these were the approximate words of Romano Guardini at the Berlin Catholic Congress of 1952, drawing a conclusion from the shattering events of the Third Reich, the Second World War, and the Marxist dictatorships that were positioning themselves for the coming decades.

Richard Schaeffler's contribution asks a still broader question: how do people exist in time, how do they secure their existence in time, and how does this happen in the sight of God, whose saving deeds are accomplished in human time? The paper, delivered in the context of the conference and also published elsewhere, falls within the scope of the theme we have already documented, for here too the key words are remembering and memorializing. It is in terms of the speech-acts and symbols of remembering that human beings construct the context of their existence. Schaeffler singles out these "achievements of memory" and juxtaposes them with the various modes of expectation. But in particular he is able to show how human memory corresponds to God's always-already-having-acted, and how human memory gives a form to the virtue of hope. Thus liturgical memorial appears not as something that is imposed on human nature: instead, it is found to possess a "natural sacramentality." Liturgiologists, of course, are in a better position than philosophers of religion to be able to demonstrate in many concrete liturgical forms, past and present, the ways in which the liturgical memorial represents a combination of "natural" and "revelation-historical" sacramentality. But even without having it pointed out to them, alert readers will recognize in the liturgies in which they participate many elements of memorial that, because they are so deeply human, have a therapeutic effect on people and at the same time, because they proclaim and praise God and his Christ in the Church, are the sacrament of salvation.

By no means was the conference able to cover the whole spectrum of possible themes, nor did it aim to do so. It is also easy to criticize much of what was presented: for example, the fact that here again the celebration of the Eucharist all too quickly becomes almost the only recognized example of liturgy, while other forms are no longer known in practice and thus recede from consciousness. But it can only detract from the highest of all possible forms (in the liturgy, this is the Eucharistic celebration) when people are not introduced to participation in the liturgy by the practice of simple forms that, at the same time, prepare us for the climactic celebration. One may say still more critically that scarcely any attention is given to a task that represents something new in contrast to the early days of the liturgical renewal—namely, the inculturation of the liturgy (the traditional liturgy, if you please) in the milieu of the North Atlantic society of our own time, together with the bitter and alarming question whether this "culture" is (still—no longer—not yet) even capable of liturgical celebration.

And in the same vein, one may note that not a word is said about one of the most urgent tasks of the Church in our country: finding and risking forms for celebrating "worship" with people who have forgotten how to pray or never learned it at all. This is not merely a situation resulting from the traditions of official atheism in the "five new federal states" in Germany. It appears that those responsible for making decisions in this regard have no significant tools for making a sensible diagnosis. But the task is there. It certainly should not frighten those who, having been taught by the first proponents of liturgical renewal, learned to know and love the riches of the liturgical tradition, when they see how wretched and impoverished the "liturgy" demanded of us must be in such a situation. But we have already said that our concern must not be with liturgy as such; we are interested in human beings in the presence of their God. That, after all, is the insight on the basis of which we can speak seriously (as we think we are doing in these pages) of "the meaning of the liturgy."

Richard Schaeffler

1. "Therefore we remember . . . ."

The Connection between Remembrance and Hope in the Present of the Liturgical Celebration. Religious-philosophical Reflections on a Religious Understanding of Time*

Introduction

"Unde et memores . . . therefore we remember" is a formula within the Eucharistic prayer, following the "narrative of institution" and locating that narrative within the context of remembrance of the death, resurrection, and ascension of Jesus. But, even though this formula appears within a specifically Christian worship service, it expresses something characteristic of services of worship in a great many, if not all religions: that memory is a part of religious celebration. We could also say that memory, when it is specifically religious in nature, has its origin in the worship celebration.

"Memores," "we are mindful" is a fundamental statement of religious consciousness as such. Before the religious individual or the religious community can begin to do or say anything, God has already spoken to it and acted upon it. God's word is always prior to human words; God's action always anticipates human action. Everything people can do or say is a response that human beings, in their speaking and acting, give to the word of God already spoken and the deed of God already done. Therefore the memory of God's word and action, which precede and make possible all human speaking and acting, belongs to the indispensable content of religious consciousness.

* First published in the "Hohenheimer Protokollen," Ostfildern, 1986.

What has just been said of religious speaking and acting in general is true in a special way of the words and actions of worship. Everything that is said and done in worship celebrations receives its content from the memory, expressed in praise, of that which God has already said and done. *Therefore memory provides the content of religious celebration.* But at the same time it must be said that *it is only in the celebration that this content of memory first attains effective presence.* For more happens in the service of worship than merely a reproduction of past events in the minds of the celebrants; what is here called to mind acquires, in the action of worship, a new and effective presence. *Only because what God has already said and done encounters the celebrants in a present and effective manner are they enabled to respond, in the worship service and in daily life, to this divine speaking and acting.* To express this in terms of the Christian Eucharistic celebration: through the effective presence of the self-surrender of Jesus not only are they enabled to remain open within the Christian community to the effects of this self-sacrifice of Jesus in themselves, but they are also able in their daily lives, through their existence in the world, through their faithful waiting in anticipation of the Lord "until he comes again," to keep the world open to the possibility of being recreated through Jesus' saving death. The "body of Christ" which believers receive in the worship service and the "body of Christ" which they as a community constitute are one and the same body that is given for many. Therefore not only the service of worship, but also the daily existence of the Christian community as the "body of Christ" mediates that self-sacrifice of Jesus to our world.

This describes a characteristic feature of religious understanding of world and time: *What has been effected by God, either in a beginning beyond all remembering or in a historical new beginning within time, and is now the object of religious memory, is something that from the point of view of the world is always approaching and is the object of hope.* But both memory and hope—memory of divine action and suffering and the hope for the recreation of the world—are really made present in the religious feast of celebration.

The Christian Eucharist, to continue this example, not only makes present that farewell meal Jesus celebrated with his disciples and the self-surrender of Jesus on the cross that it symbolically anticipates, but prefigures what the community hopes to celebrate as a "heavenly wedding banquet" at the end of days, which Jesus himself promised, describing it as "eating with Abraham, Isaac, and Jacob in the kingdom of heaven" (Matt 8:11). And the Eucharistic celebration can symbolically prefigure this heavenly wedding banquet because Jesus' farewell meal was already just such a symbolic anticipation. "I will never again drink of the fruit of the vine until that day when I drink it new in my Father's kingdom" (Mark 14:25; Matt 26:29). Thus the memory of the cross and the hopeful expectation of the heavenly banquet do not constitute two originally separate elements that have been secondarily joined in the Christian Eucharistic celebration; for in Jesus' farewell supper also the symbolic prefiguring of his death on the cross and the saying about "drinking wine in the kingdom of the Father" were not two originally separate elements that Jesus (or the narrator of the last supper account) secondarily and superficially combined. This internal connection appears more clearly when we take note of the fact that the content of both elements—Jesus' self-surrender on the cross and his eternal glory can be celebrated in the form of a meal.

Abraham, Isaac, and Jacob, and all those who will sit at table with them in the reign of God do not receive two different gifts, connected only at a secondary level: on the one hand, community with God as the heavenly father of the household and host, and on the other hand, some kind of heavenly food and drink as the external expression of divine hospitality. This description would, of course, fit any meal to which human beings invite their friends. But being invited to God's table— and this is a hoped-for saving event in a wide variety of religions of various peoples and therefore an equally widespread practice in worship—means something different. It is the one and indivisible event in which human beings receive their life from the fullness of the godhead.

Human beings can never possess their own existence out of their own abundance; they must allow it to be given to them anew every day. We do not eat our "daily bread" once and for all, but must receive it again every day; we do not breathe in the life-giving air once and for all, but constantly, again and again. Eating and drinking and breathing are, in each instance, a renewed receiving of life, which will never be our enduring possession, but must continually be received anew as gift. Thus the question arises how this external gift of food and drink, of breath and other "necessities of life" can become our intimate possession and the source of our life. The answer found in many religions is: it is only possible because all these gifts are ways of experiencing, through our senses, how our earthly, human life is given to us out of the fullness of God's life.

Only a God can give in such a way as not to give us merely *something* (which would presuppose that we, as the recipients, are already there), but so as to give us our own existence and life. And only a God can give in such a way as to give not merely a handout, something that God simply possesses, but so that God in person, in the fullness of divine life, becomes the gift. God's own breath, the Bible says, which means God's own life, is "breathed into the nostrils" of the human being, and the human becomes a living being. Thus life, even in the daily experience of our earthly existence, is the continually new reception of God's self-gift for the many. Air, water and earth, and the products that grow upon the earth are therefore, religiously understood, visible forms that mediate God's self-gift to us. To that extent every meal in which we participate has something sacramental about it.

The heavenly banquet, however, is the completion of what we anticipate symbolically in every earthly meal: the perfected reception of human life from the abundance of divine life. And Jesus' self-surrender for many anticipates that completion within time. His body that was sacrificed for us, is "real food," "the bread of life," and therefore already that food that will some day be eaten at table with Abraham, Isaac, and Jacob: the fullness of divine self-gift that gives us humans the fullness of life. "Whoever eats of this bread will live forever" (John 6:51, and frequently). Thus because God's final, eschatological self-surrender for the life of the world is anticipated in Jesus' self-surrender on the cross, the heavenly banquet can also be anticipated symbolically in the Eucharistic celebration, in the memorial of the Lord's suffering. And therefore memory and hope become one in the celebration of worship and are combined in a single present, the hour of the feast.

The following considerations will address the question of the way in which memory and hope are brought together in the present hour of worship, how this is possible, and what it means. In the first part of what follows, we will propose a general philosophical notion about the nature of memory and its relationship to anticipation in human life. In the second part, we will speak of the specifically religious meaning of memory and its connection with hopeful anticipation. Finally, we will redirect our attention to the worship celebration in order to test whether general philosophical and specifically religious-philosophical considerations can contribute anything to a better understanding of what it means to say that in the hour of worship the remembered past and the hoped-for future are joined in a single present.

I. Memory and the Synthesis of Events to Form Experience

Let me begin with a note on the history of philosophy that may appear to many as an expression of philosophical erudition that could well be dispensed with. A few stages farther along we will be attempting to pursue some ideas of Immanuel Kant, although in a very simple manner. Kant made the observation that "experience" is more than a mere collection of impressions. Experience is, in fact, an orderly construction that allows us to orient ourselves and enables us to draw conclusions, providing us with criteria for selecting and evaluating the things that are important and deserve our attention. Such a construction does not appear of itself; we have to build it. And all the individual impressions we receive become building blocks for that construction. Kant expressed this in vivid terms: "We have to spell out events in order to be able to read them as experience." The individual events that impress us are like letters from which we must construct a readable text.

There are, as we now know, "dyslexics," people who understand letters but cannot build words and sentences from them. For them, grasping the elements does not produce a constructed context; recognition of the letters yields no text. There are also, we must add, "experiential dyslexics," people who register countless impressions but are incapable of constructing a context within which they all make sense. Kant's question, which must be posed here in very simple terms, addressed this problem: *What must we do to move from appearances to an orderly context of experience; to organize letters into a readable text?* An important partial answer would be that, together with other elements, the powers of memory play a role, especially those that differ from one another but together combine in contstructing a context:

Three Powers of Memory

It is our task to recognize, among our various impressions, *those that are similar* (= 1.), against that background to distinguish new things as clearly new, and finally to combine the constants and variables found in our experience by the application of concepts. Primary among these are the concepts of thing (or person) and quality, of cause and effect. We attribute variable qualities to an enduring person or thing, and explain variable events or appearances as the result of new combinations of a few, constant complexes of causes. This task is controlled by the idea of the "world," that is, by the conscious purpose of constructing, out of the abundance of our impressions, an orderly whole within which each individual item must find its unchangeable, clear, and distinct place.

It is our task to *discover ourselves* (= 2.) among our shifting experiences, so that we may construct, out of the abundance of stories we could tell, that one story of our own individual and social life that allows us to attribute that abundance of experiences to ourselves as their "subjects." This task is controlled by the idea of the "self," that is, by the conscious purpose of discovering within our shifting life-situations the one characteristic way in which we have appropriated the external circumstances and their changes as *our own story*; how, in an equally characteristic way, we may have failed in that task; or how we have lost ourselves in the flood of events and retrieved ourselves from it.

These two tasks, of building an orderly world out of the abundance of our impressions, and of constructing a unified life story out of the fullness of our experiences, appear at first glance to be purely formal. The concepts of "orderly whole" as applied to the world, and of "historical unit" as applied to the self tell us nothing about the content of the things that are to be drawn together in such a whole or unit, nor do they tell us what particular form that whole or unit can take. Therefore these two formal tasks are supplemented by a third, related to content: the task of *extracting* from the abundance of our impressions and experiences *certain pieces of content as "memorable"* (= 3.), things that can serve as crystallization points for the synthesis of our experience. These include *moments of identification*, to which an abundance of later experiences can be related because in those moments, as if in a focused beam of light, we have understood who we ourselves are and what is the condition of our world. Such memorable moments also include *crisis events* in light of which "our world collapsed" (i.e., the context within which we have thus far interpreted and evaluated our experiences lost its power of orientation), so that we "no longer knew who we were" (i.e., how we can appropriate such experiences as parts of our own life story, so that we can recognize ourselves in them). Finally, such memorable moments include *experiences of restoration* of the self and the world (i.e., events from which the wholeness of our context of experience and the unity of our self and its history have emerged in an altered form).

An Example

I will venture to give an example of this third task—that of isolating what is memorable from the abundance of what is remembered. This example has for me the character of an identification experience. I can never forget a scene from my first year of school, when a fellow pupil had committed some offense or other against his school obligations (it may have been some homework he had not done) and tried to justify it with an excuse (I no longer remember what he said; let us suppose he said that he had had to help his parents with the harvest on their farm). What I cannot forget is the fact that the teacher did not believe his excuse. I was utterly horrified at the time. First I was shocked at the total powerlessness of a person whose word is not believed. As I foresaw, every attempt to make the rejected excuse plausible by embellishments only made the hearer (in this case, the teacher) more skeptical. If he were taken to be a liar, even in this one concrete situation, his attempts to justify himself would appear to be more lies. Every attempt to say another word was therefore useless. And there arose in me a rage against the teacher who, by her suspicion, had silenced my fellow pupil, even though he continued to try to say something. But suddenly a doubt arose in me: could the teacher be right? Did she perhaps know that the boy was really not busy harvesting on the previous day? Had she seen him, maybe, far away from his father's fields, without his noticing her?

I was horrified again because the teacher's suspicion, which had just aroused my anger, was now stirring within me, even though only as a mild doubt. I do not remember how the story of the teacher and the pupil ended. But the feeling of helplessness remains deeply engraved in my memory, for I had seen that not only when a person is really lying, and not only when one is unjustly suspected, but even when we cannot know whether she or he is speaking the truth every word is useless, every answer is questionable, and all speech dies, so that the speaker, the person spoken to, and all those within earshot are silenced and stand dumb and isolated in space.

Although at the time I was incapable of giving adequate expression in words to what I had experienced, from my present perspective I think that the deep shock I then felt arose from the fact that in this one, accidental event I discovered something about the world and myself. The world is the kind of place where lies happen; the world is such that in individual cases one cannot know whether a word that is spoken is truth or lie; the world is a place where suspicion can have a foundation, but also where groundless suspicion cannot be refuted; the world is such that speakers are silenced, even though they may be speaking the truth, because lies are possible and therefore suspicion is irrefutable.

And who am I, myself, in this world? I am someone who does not want to be silent, alone, powerless in face of others' suspicion. Therefore I am someone who desires that words will find answers, that dialogue will not be broken off, that trust will be maintained. And I am someone who, in his desire for word and truth, touches the frontiers of powerlessness, who cannot change the fact that, in this world, lies are possible and trust can be violated, and therefore that suspicion stalks me as well. I, with my will toward word and truth, am powerless, just as that pupil was before his teacher and, as I also vaguely sensed, the teacher before her pupil.

The story I have just told not only became part of my life story, but remained with me as something like an identification experience. When I think back on it, even today, it tells me something about what my world is like and how I fit into it. It would, of course, be a mistake to identify one's whole understanding of self and world in terms of such individual experiences. There are certainly many stories that must be told if one wants to tell one's own life story. And yet I think that the unity of our life story achieves its form for us in the process of selecting, from an abundance of memories, a limited number of those "memorable moments" in which we can picture for ourselves in a vivid and exemplary way our identity, the crises of that identity, and its changes as it takes on newer forms.

Three Forms of Anticipation

The three powers of memory of which we have just spoken correspond to three forms of anticipation.

The first task was that of connecting the constants and variables in our impressions by the use of concepts. This task of memory corresponds to a specific form of anticipation called *prognosis* (= 1.) Our success or failure in the tasks of perceiving as constant those things or persons in terms of which we interpret the multiplicity of our impressions as changing characteristics of those constants, and of discovering the complex of stable causes on the basis of whose changing combinations we explain the variables in our impressions is affirmed when we are able to derive predictions from these interpretations and explanations, and when the actual course of events confirms or refutes those predictions. The construction of theories in the empirical sciences and the testing of such theories on the basis of confirmed or disproved prognoses is the prime example of this process.

The second task of memory consists in combining the multiplicity of our experiences to form a unified life story. This task of memory corresponds to a particular form of anticipation, namely, the awareness of a *twofold obligation* (= 2.): the obligation always to remain true to ourselves in everything we do or suffer, and the obligation to trust in this identity of ours as we make our way into the unknown. Without the courage to face the unknown, the fullness of our experiences would yield no story, but only a set of variations on a single theme. But without fidelity to ourselves the story would not be *our* life story; we could not rediscover our own identity in it and we would not be able to appropriate the fullness of all that we have experienced as *ours*, as belonging to our own identity. However, the awareness of this twofold obligation implies a *hope* that what we cannot achieve by force will be given us: that we will not lose ourselves, but instead will find ourselves when we squander ourselves, out of sensitivity to unforeseeable tasks, for the sake of the demanding opportunities provided by our life-situation.

The third task of memory is to isolate from the abundance of our impressions and experiences those "memorable moments"—in the sense of identification experiences, crisis events, or moments of the restoration of our world and our self in newer form—that spotlight and clarify for us our own situation and that of our world.

This task of memory also corresponds to a special form of anticipation: *confidence* (= 3.) that events of this kind, while they will change and deepen their meaning in the course of our lives, will never lose their power of orientation. They change their meaning, because over the years they are filled with new content, they make new statements. This is because our constant interpretation of new experiences in light of these "memorable moments" repeatedly sheds new light on them as well. Nevertheless, they do not lose their power of orientation. As they help us to understand anew even what was unforeseen, they themselves also acquire, in ever changing ways, the possibility of new interpretation and understanding.

II. Memory and Anticipation: A Religious Understanding

The Uniqueness of What Is "Memorable" in Religion

The specifically religious meaning of memory is especially evident in the third task: that of isolating the memorable moments from the multiplicity of individual and group experiences.

Identification experiences have a special character in a religious context: they are interpreted as *experiences of participation*. Those events that are told again and again by religious people, because new individual experiences can always be interpreted in light of them, are here not primarily incidents in one's individual life, but events of divine action and suffering, such that all human experiences are understood as the outgrowth and present forms of those same events. In light of the action and suffering of a divinity, human beings interpret their own deeds and sufferings as aspects of participation in that which a divine being has previously done and suffered.

Crisis events, when religiously understood, have the character of *experiences of judgment*. Memorable moments of this type must be told again and again because those moments in which human life crashes against its limits recall to religious people that their sharing in the life of the divinity is threatened by a deep ambivalence. The human being repeats the divine creative word "with unclean lips" and shapes "with unclean hands" a human image of the divine work of salvation. For when all the truth in human words and all the effects of human action are traced to the fact that, in human words and actions, the creative word of the divinity and the divine saving action and suffering are revived, then at the same time it is clear that no one is so much in danger of becoming a sinner as the one who feels called to such a share in God's speaking and acting. And no one in this situation can hope to be justified in any other way than by accepting God's judgment on him- or herself and trusting, under that judgment, the saving grace of God.

This, then, is the meaning of religiously-understood incidents of the restoration of the self and the world. These are *experiences of pure grace in the hour of judgment*. Nearly all religions have purification rituals that are meant to enable people to symbolize the effective presence of God in the world without sinning against the divine holiness. It is no accident that the form of these purification rituals is often closely related to that of death rituals. Immersion in water, going through a narrow gate, or sprinkling the person with blood are especially frequent signs employed in these rites. Human beings cannot become capable of *participation* in the action and suffering of a divinity, and thereby of a religiously-understood self-discovery, except by subjecting themselves to the fatal *judgment* of that divinity, so that thereby they can overcome the impurity of their hearts and hands and allow themselves to be restored to a *life under God's protection*.

Crisis events and those in which the individual or social self-consciousness finds itself renewed in a process of movement through such crises belong, as was said earlier, to the "memorable moments" in the life of every human being and every human society. Such memorable moments are told again and again because new, individual experiences can be repeatedly interpreted in light of those moments. But as far as the religious consciousness is concerned, it is true that those events that must be told again and again because the crises of individual lives interpreted in light of them are, for the most part, not incidents in the lives of individual human beings, but the events of divine action and suffering. A god has removed, by the god's own death, all the impurity with which human lips and hands are stained. And wherever human beings—in their daily lives and in the cultic symbols that are ordered to the interpretation of those lives—"enter through the narrow gate, descend into the killing and revivifying bath of water, are consecrated to a renewal of life with the blood of sacrificed animals" they understand the event, which they experience as the crisis and restoration of their life, as a sharing in that which the divine being has previously done and suffered. It is this action and suffering of the divine, and not primarily their own fate, that religious individuals and societies narrate again and again, because through these truly "memorable" events they interpret everything that has happened in their own lives and everything that will happen in the future.

Christians also tell their life stories, as does the Christian community, as a series of events reflecting Jesus' way of the cross as his road to glory. The primary theme of such a narrative is therefore not the religious person and the religious community, but the dying and rising of Jesus. Of course, the life of believers is also interpreted in light of this "memorable event." "If any want to become my followers, let them deny themselves and take up their cross daily and follow me" (Luke 9:23). The event that forms the content of Christians' religious memory consisted, as far as human experience is concerned, in people's having denied Jesus and demanded that Pilate sentence him to crucifixion. ". . . you handed [him] over and rejected [him] in the presence of Pilate" (Acts 3:13). In the memory of this event Christians interpret *all the crisis events of their lives* in such a way that those crises challenge them to accept the sentence pronounced on Jesus as a sentence pronounced on them and thus to take up "their cross" (which always means their condemnation). Human beings are called to appropriate the charge that brought about that condemnation as a charge against themselves, and so to deny themselves. But the same event that in human experience consisted of people's having denied Jesus and condemned him to crucifixion consists also, for Christian faith, in God's having raised the Crucified from the dead and made him "the Author of life" ("the Author of life, whom God raised from the dead," Acts 3:15). Christians interpret those crisis experiences in life that draw them into following Jesus' way of the cross as, at the same time, experiences of *restoration to new life*, because the "Author of life" they are to follow on the way of the cross is also the one who opens to human beings the ways of life by traveling those ways before them.

Therefore the religious memory of Jesus' cross and resurrection corresponds to a confidence that points toward the future: the confidence that in all the crisis experiences of our lives in which we fail in our duty to reflect and mediate God's saving actions in this world we will encounter the Son of God who has taken upon himself, as our representative, the judgment under which we stand and who challenges us to follow his way under the cross and thus to gain a share in his glory.

The Unity of the Self and the Continuity of Its History

Religious individuals and groups, as we have said, understand all the content of their lives in such a way that in all human action and suffering the powerful salvation and freely accepted suffering of a divine being is reflected and newly present in ever new and unpredictable ways, so that it makes its meaning known to us in aspects that are always new and surprising. Therefore interpreting the religious memory of Jesus' cross and resurrection means narrating the whole history of Christian life. Only when the stories of individual Christians and of all Christianity have reached their end, when all situations have been endured in which human beings find themselves standing under God's judgment and are required to take that judgment upon themselves, renouncing themselves: only then will it be clear what it means to say that wherever human beings experience themselves as sinners subject to God's judgment they encounter the one who "for our sake has become sin."

And only when all the forms in which human beings know that they have been endowed with new life through God's grace have been experienced with gratitude will it be clear what it means to say that wherever renewal of life is given them they encounter the Lord who has been raised from the dead. This also means that telling the story of Christian life means interpreting the one saving deed that God has done in Jesus' cross and resurrection. The unity of the self, the "I" (the religious individual) and the group, the "we" (the religious community) which contains the multiplicity of experiences that make up an individual or community history is, in a religious understanding, the unity of a divine act of salvation that is reflected and renewed in all the shifting events of this life. And that awareness of this unity of the self or the group is, religiously understood, the continually renewed preservation of the hope of encountering again, in all the changing situations of individual and community life, the God who has done this saving work.

Of course, this re-encounter is, religiously understood, not simply a "conceptual recognition," not merely a combination of various items in our consciousness and the emphasis on their similarity; it is, rather, "calling upon the Name." And that means that it is an entry into a mutual relationship that draws together all the changing situations of human life into the unity of a life story; therefore that story has its abiding center in the encounter with God and derives its continuity from that encounter. Hence the trust implied in religious memory can also be described as follows: even when "heaven and earth pass away," that is, when the whole theoretical and practical framework by which human experience is oriented collapses, religious people maintain a confident hope that they will be able, in a new heaven and a new earth, to call the old God by the old Name. The mutual relationship into which human beings enter when they call God by name and thus acknowledge God as the one who has already appropriated every human deed and suffering as God's own divine work and suffering creates the unity of the story that the religious individual and, in particular, the religious community can tell as its own story—even if they cannot recognize themselves in such a changed world. It is enough that they find their God again in this changed world, and in the encounter with God, in calling God by name, they find themselves again.

One may even call it a distinguishing mark of the divine that what a god does or suffers, and what therefore constitutes the substance of religious memory, becomes a "name" by which this god can be called in any future, no matter how unexpected: you are the one who created the world by your word; you are the one who made for yourself a people out of those who were enslaved to strange gods (e.g., Egyptian god-kings); you are the one who, by your commandment, leads people to freedom. Or, in Christian terms: you are the one who raised Jesus from the dead and who will lead those who believe in Jesus into communion with Jesus' death and resurrection. That this Name will remain when heaven and earth pass away, that the religious person and the religious community will be able to call upon this same God by the same name, beyond all the collapses and restorations of "heaven and earth": this is the confident hope in which individual and community find assurance. But it is just that assurance based on hope that in biblical language is called "faith." "Now faith is the assurance of things hoped for" (Heb 11:1). And this assurance in hope gives religious people the confidence that enables them not to lose their identity when they can no longer perceive the basis on which they can found their sure orientation in face of the radical changes in their history. This "assurance of things hoped for" is also, as the Letter to the Hebrews says, "a conviction of things not seen."

III. Memory and Anticipation in the Present of Divine Worship

The state of the problem

Memory, as we have seen, has always been connected with anticipation, both within and outside the religious context, and the manifold forms of memory correspond to equally manifold forms of anticipation. This is true also of religious memory and the hopeful confidence that goes with it. It is insufficient to describe this connection between memory and anticipation simply as a psychic process, something that takes place at a conscious level and is consciously directed. That would presuppose that the self first exists as a unified reality and that it then combines the various things that arise in its consciousness to form an orderly whole. But we have seen earlier in the line of thought we are now pursuing that the combination of the remembered past and the expected future, while occurring in the consciousness, at the same time takes place in such a way that the unity of that consciousness *as a historical entity* only emerges from this process of combination.

What we mean when we say "I" or "we" is an identity of our self-understanding that only arises because we are capable of telling our story *as ours*. And in the second, religious-philosophical part of the considerations being presented here it became clear that in religious consciousness the remembered past and expected future can only be combined because that religious consciousness achieves its identity *in an act of encounter*. Religious memory is not exhausted in reactivating the residual memories of earlier experiences; and religious anticipation is not exhausted in the ability to construct an imaginary future, i.e., in the power of fantasy to suggest ideas of coming events. For the present in which the remembered past and expected future are combined *in such a way* that the religious I and we that can tell their stories only emerge from that combination is a special kind of present: it is not brought forth in an abstract act of thought or in the pure interiority of imagination, but in the speech-act of calling upon a name, in which the human being enters a correlative relationship with God and in that encounter experiences the saving actions of God, accomplished long ago, as something present, and in such a way that thereby the saving actions of God that are hoped for in the future appear symbolically, but as effective also in the present.

"Deus, cuius antiqua miracula etiam nostris temporibus coruscare sentimus" ("O God, we see your wonderful deeds of old shine forth even to our own day"): these are the community's words in a prayer spoken to their God in the Easter Vigil. At the same time, it acknowledges that in its encounter with God the most distant future of its story is already anticipated. Therefore it can add to its present appeal to the God who led Israel out of Egypt the trusting petition "that all the peoples of the earth may be numbered among the offspring of Abraham"—a *transire*, a "passing over" in which Israel's *transitus* through the Red Sea will for the first time receive the full measure of its saving significance.

Our reflections have returned to the starting point: the worship service, the remembered past and anticipated future that are gathered up in the present of the celebration. From one important perspective this union of past and future has now become easier to understand. For the unity of the religious I and we, on the basis of which the world of experience is shaped into an orderly and religiously-interpreted whole, was constituted, as we have said, by the speech-act of calling on the Name. And the whole lifetime of individual believers and their community achieves its cohesion not through the dependable course of the stars that enables us to count days and years, but through the fidelity of God who, as the doer of those "wonderful deeds of old," is also present to our appeal even now, thus furnishing a basis for our confidence that even in the farthest future God will encounter us as the agent of the same saving actions, and will again be known and be called by name: "Let the name of the Lord be praised, from henceforth now and forever." In the fidelity of God who will be called by name even in the farthest reaches of the future, time (that is, the context of all the events in the life of a human being and of the world) achieves its unity, and the life of believers and of the community acquires its historical continuity.

From this point of view we can understand that calling on the name of God has a central place in worship. It would be an interesting task for philosophers of language to give a more precise description to the gathering up of remembered past and anticipated future in the linguistic form of "calling on the Name." But at this point our subject is not prayer as speech-act, but the sacraments as symbolic actions. Within the scope of this paper we can approach this subject only from a restricted point of view, but one chosen with the intention of enabling the specifically Christian meaning of the combination of remembered past and anticipated future to emerge.

At this point, we must frankly admit, the philosopher of religion is overstepping his or her responsibility. Therefore what will be attempted in the following reflections can only be a suggestion for theologians. It is they who must decide whether these considerations describe what is distinctively Christian in the sacraments and characterize the combination of memory and hope that is accomplished in the sacraments in a specifically Christian way. But it is at least worth the attempt to test whether general religious-philosophical considerations, like those already proposed, can open up a context within which the special character of what is distinctively Christian can be illuminated.

The drawing together of remembered past and hoped-for future in "sealing with the Spirit," or the natural and supernatural sacramentality of human life.

We ordinarily speak of an "irremovable seal" or "indelible character" that the Holy Spirit places in the souls of believers in connection with baptism, confirmation, and orders. But in what follows our interest is not in the individual theology of these three sacraments, still less in a particular interpretation of the "sacramental character" they impart. Our concern is, by use of this example, to make clear what is meant by the special relation of memory and hope, of remembered past and anticipated future.

Biblical language about the "Spirit" and its "communication" to human beings must not be understood "pneumatically" from the outset, in the Greek sense of a contrast of spirit and body, and only secondarily in the sense of the Pauline contrast of "spirit" and "flesh." The communication of the divine Spirit to human beings is always, in the first instance, that communication of the divine breath of life to Adam, the consequence of which is that human beings in a quite literal sense "with every intake of breath" receive their whole existence from the divine abundance and return it to God with every exhalation. Thus, in taking and giving, they share in the life of God. Hence a sacramental communication of the divine Spirit is not a supernatural addition to the gift of natural life, but its elevation to a new way of living from and for God.

The Spirit thus received as the breath of life is also, for human beings, the vehicle of the word. With our exhaled breath we send forth in words what is within us: our views, our insights, our intentions. And because the breath of life that conveys our word is something already breathed into us by God, the word that we speak also returns to God, so that it reaches God's ear as praise. And as our exhaled breath goes forth irretrievably into illimitable space, our word also, once it has been spoken, goes out into the immeasurable. Biblically speaking, it invites all other beings who have been given the breath of life to join with our word: "let all that has breath praise the Lord." Thus the sacramental communication of the divine Spirit is not a supernatural addition to the gift of the natural word, but its elevation to a new way of responding with our whole existence to God's word of creation.

As life turned outward, as word spoken into the unlimited, the Spirit makes public what is within us. Without such expression, our internal self would remain hidden. "For what human being knows what is truly human except the human spirit that is within?" (1 Cor 2:11). With this reflection on the hiddenness of what is in the human being the concept of spirit acquires a new level of meaning. Whereas life expresses itself necessarily—so that we cannot avoid exhaling the breath of life that makes us alive—the expression of the spirit is a free action.

Still more: if that which is to be communicated freely is now seen as our essential internal self and therefore something hidden, the question arises whether the word we express can have the power to communicate this internal self, that which irreplaceably belongs to the human being, to other ears. Paul, from whose First Letter to the Corinthians we have taken the passage just quoted, discusses this question not only in view of "that which is within the human being," but particularly with regard to "that which God is." But the analogy with the human spirit which alone is able to know what the human being is enables the apostle also to say of God: "So also no one comprehends what is truly God's except the Spirit of God" (*ibid.*). At this point the question of how it is possible that the free expression of God can make God's internal being—Paul calls it "the depths of God"—intelligible to an external hearer becomes extremely acute. Paul answers it in a surprising way. To hear and understand that word, the hearers must receive a share in that very divine Spirit who alone knows the depths of the Godhead. "Now we have received . . . the Spirit that is from God, so that we may understand the gifts bestowed on us by God" (1 Cor 2:12).

Just as all human life is a sharing in divine life and originates with the communication of the divine breath to the human being, so all human knowledge is that which God's free grace desires and freely communicates, a sharing in the divine Spirit, and originates in the fact that God communicates not only God's word, but the divine Spirit—the way in which God alone knows God—to human beings.

Everything that later theology would call "supernatural revelation" differs from "natural knowledge of God" not only because God freely communicates to human beings matters that they could not know by their own abilities, but because the "Spirit" who "knows what is truly God's," and therefore belongs to the irreplaceable "internal being" of the divine self-understanding, is imparted to human beings. Just as we, as living beings, naturally share in the divine breath of life that enlivens everything, so by God's free choice we share in the divine Spirit who "searches everything, even the depths of God" (1 Cor 2:10). From this point of view the sacramental communication of the divine Spirit is a "supernatural event" because it enables us to speak about God not "in words . . . taught by human wisdom," but, sharing in God's Spirit, "taught by the Spirit, interpreting spiritual things to those who are spiritual" (1 Cor 2:13), that is, the things that of themselves belong to the knowledge of God.

Every word uttered in preaching or the message of faith recorded in Sacred Scripture only speaks to our spirit, is only heard and understood by us, if it recalls to us this event of the communication of the Spirit and enables us to hope that, in all the future experiences of our lives, we will find only a new way of interpreting this one word, this one self-communication of the divine Spirit and God's plan of salvation.

But because God is faithful, that plan of salvation is irrevocable. It is a "yes" without any "no" that was revealed, as the apostle says, in Jesus' self-surrender on behalf of many: "the Son of God, Jesus Christ, . . . was not 'Yes and No;' but in him it is always 'Yes' " (2 Cor 1:19). This yes without any no that God has spoken to us in the Son is different from the word that we ourselves can utter, because, as we have seen, religious consciousness interprets every crisis in its own history in which the unity of the self collapses and the wholeness of the world crumbles as the expression of its standing under God's judgment. Called in all our deeds and sufferings to be figures in which God's saving action is imaged anew, we find that we are performing our service "with unclean lips and hands." Thus in our own selves we are both "yes" and "no." We must say "yes" to our own life if we are to appropriate our story as our own; and we must say "no" to ourselves if we admit that we have failed in our task. In this "yes" and "no" the unity of our religious consciousness collapses, and we can reconcile ourselves neither with God nor with our own life.

Christian faith does not relieve us from this "no." "If any want to become my followers, let them deny themselves and take up their cross"—the judgment pronounced upon them. But because this "denial of self" can be interpreted as "following Christ," as the image and present form of the judgment that Jesus accepted for himself as representative for many, the "yes" of divine grace has already been spoken for us also, within the "no" of judgment. This divine "yes" is now the new breath of life that fills us, the new spirit that insures us a share in the divine Spirit and enables us in the midst of our experience of judgment to call our loving God by name. "When we cry 'Abba! Father!' it is that very Spirit bearing witness with our spirit that we are children of God" (Rom 8:15-16).

Therefore the communication of the divine Spirit that enables us to hear and understand God's "yes" is the "seal" that is impressed on our soul and "establishes us" (2 Cor 1:21-22). In this divine Spirit we are "marked with a seal for the day of redemption" (Eph 4:30). All Christian memory and anticipation is therefore "established" in the always newly present expectation that our spirit is a sharing in the divine Spirit and that God's "constancy," God's faithfulness, is irrevocable.

The gift of life that we receive and give back with every breath, and the gift of the word that we utter and promulgate with our breath of life, creating community between speaker and hearers and inviting "everything that has breath" to common life, is the basis for all the "natural" or "universal" sacramentality of human life. For our life and our word are the sensibly perceptible, always newly present effective signs of our sharing in the divine Spirit. Life, in receiving and giving, is a sharing in the life of God whose life-giving exhalation of the Spirit is a self-gift to creatures that enables them in their breathing and speaking to give themselves, together with God, to "every living thing." Therefore religious memory of the divine act of creation in which we received the breath of life is joined with the hopeful anticipation that the word we speak with our whole heart will reach countless beings and unite them with us in the praise of God, because this word, borne by our life's breath, our whole being, carries with it the life bestowed on us by the divine Spirit and bears it outward to all creatures, who, like us, have received the breath of life from the mouth of God.

However, all "special" or "supernatural" sacramentality is founded in the self-communication of the divine Spirit by which God in a free act (not predetermined by the free decision to create us in the first place) conveys to us the divine plan of salvation, which also is freely chosen and not predetermined by our creaturely nature. This occurs in an external word that, however, can only be understood by us because God at the same time gives us a share in the divine self-knowledge, that is, in the divine Spirit.

The "supernatural sacramentality" of our lives comes from the fact that with this divine "yes" or "no," with this "communication of the divine Spirit to our spirits" we are "marked with a seal for the day of redemption." Sacraments are present forms in which this sharing in the divine Spirit, this state of being founded on the divine "yes" that we are enabled to repeat in our own lives, is continually given to us anew. And that "sacramental character," the "sacramental sealing with the Spirit" is an effective present sign of the self-communication of the divine Spirit and of its constancy that will support us to the end of our days.

Unde et memores—therefore we remember

"Unde et memores . . . therefore we remember," as we recalled at the outset, is a formula drawn from the Eucharistic prayer, but also a fundamental statement of religious thinking as such. Memory, as we have discovered in the course of these reflections, is what makes it possible both within and outside of religious contexts for us to narrate the multiplicity of our experiences *as our own story* and thus to arrive at our own identity, the unity of our individual "I" and our social "we" *each within its own history*. In a religious context, this constitutive meaning of memory as that which grounds the I and the we derives from the fact that religious persons understand all their actions and suffering as the ever renewed present forms in which the saving deeds and sufferings of a divinity achieve effective presence for them. This memory, that is, this ever newly present experience of that which has already been effected by the deity, is combined with the hopeful confidence that in all the future changing situations of life the same god and the same saving work will be encountered in ever new forms. Thus religious memory also anticipates the most distant future we can hope for.

This re-encounter with God and God's saving work is not a merely psychic process, not merely the reproduction of remembered images and their combination with fantasies of future events; it is the entry into a relationship through calling on a name. All continuity in individual and social history is thus founded on the hope that that name "abides, even though heaven and earth disappear." Only this confidence allows religious people to organize the very different and unforeseeable events of their lives within a context in which they acquire meaning for the subject. Only in the power of this hope can they "spell appearances in order to be able to read them as religious experience." Only this unity of memory and hope constitutes for the religious consciousness the wholeness of a world of experience (even beyond all historical catastrophes) and the unity of a self-consciousness (even when, beholding itself, it no longer recognizes itself in its own deeds and sufferings).

Finally, however, the source of this unity of the I or we and this wholeness of the world of experience, as religiously interpreted, has become clear: calling on the divine Name, whereby religious persons enter into correlation with God and thereby gain endurance and constancy for their lives is, in turn, founded on the self-communication of the divine Spirit. For all the words we speak are uttered with our breath of life and therefore return the life-giving breath of God, by which we were called into existence, in an expression of praise to God. On this rests what we can call the "natural sacramentality" of human life: our life as a whole is an image of the divine gift of the breath of life. Our whole utterance is an image of the divine word that is "placed in our souls" with that breath. Therefore our word is capable of interpreting all the changing circumstances of life as images of the divine acts of salvation.

However, all "special" or "supernatural sacramentality" rests on the fact that, according to Christian conviction, all the crises of our lives have already been anticipated by the judgment that Jesus took upon himself as representative for many. In remembering Jesus' cross, the Christian repeats God's "no"—the "no" that God has spoken in judging sinners. Christians "deny themselves and take up their cross," the judgment spoken against them, "daily." In remembering Jesus' resurrection, however, Christians speak God's "yes without any no," uttered in the Son as God's forgiving Word. And Christians can repeat this "yes without any no" spoken by God because they have received and been "sealed with" the Spirit.

This communication of the divine Spirit, this sealing of our spirit with the Spirit of God, creates the present in which we can call God again and again by the name "Father," and in so calling on God unite the memory of God's saving deeds already done with the anticipation of our coming redemption. In this present the unity of our I and we is continually renewed, the unity that makes it possible for us to narrate all the acts and sufferings of our lives as our story: the story of those who have lost themselves in guilt and received themselves again as gift, as sons and daughters of God, through the communication of the divine Spirit.

"Spelling appearances in order to be able to read them as experience" means for Christians, in the sacramentally bestowed community with God's Spirit, to read all the events of our lives as the one "commentary" on the one "word" in which, in the midst of the "no" spoken over us in judgment, God's irrevocable "yes" has been uttered and can be repeated by us in the spirit of divine sonship and daughterhood.

"Unde et memores . . . donec veniat: therefore we remember . . . until he comes again." Memory and hopeful anticipation and confidence are joined in the present celebration of the sacrament that seals us with this Spirit.

Clemens Thoma, s.v.d.

2. Memorial of Salvation: The Celebration of Faith in Judaism

Near the end of the First World War, Franz Rosenzweig (1886–1929) wrote to his Christian "sparring partner" Eugen Rosenstock (1888–1973) that "the pious person, then . . . as Jew or Christian is something quite different, even opposite, although correlative opposites like two bone sutures knit together (that is, one in the sight of God, but in human eyes directly contrary). But behind, or rather within this twofold appearance there is the same metal. The sanctities themselves are different, the ultimate root within the soul . . . is the same; identical with reference to the paganism of 'secular piety.'"[1] What we want to do today is to discover this "common metal" that constitutes, or could and should constitute the fundamental stratum in the souls of Jews and Christians.

However, the subject of divine worship has so many meanings in Judaism and Christianity, it is so manifold and so intimate, that it can only be approached and pursued a little way, while never being comprehended as a whole. For the sake of simplicity and relative clarity we will begin in the period immediately after the composition of the Old Testament (2nd century B.C.E.), conscious of the fact that all Jewish ideas and forms of divine worship received their decisive impulse from biblical worship as practiced in the Temple. First we will discuss early Jewish and early rabbinic ideas of divine worship (I), then

[1] Franz Rosenzweig, *Gesammelte Schriften: Briefe und Tagebücher* 1 (Haag, 1979) 316.

40

the worship of God as the carrying out of the covenant (II), and finally some practical liturgical suggestions for the forms of Christian worship (III).

I. Early Jewish and Early Rabbinic Ideas of Divine Worship

In the post-Old Testament period there emerge two basic types of Jewish liturgical worship that are constantly in correlation: a more *vertical* form that emphasizes the line from the worshipping community *upward* to the throne of God, and a more *horizontal* form that stresses the line connecting past and future with the present.

1. The Vertical Type of Worship

The worship service that emphasizes a relational movement upward from below (and then also downward from above) was based on early Jewish esoteric thought (the cryptic features of religious and practical worship practices) of the Temple priests and their successors. The religious esoteric of the early Jews can be precisely dated from the eighth century B.C.E. (Isa 6:1-3; Ezek 1, 8; Dan 7:9). Various early Jewish worshipping communities interpreted their liturgical practices in relation to and as variations of the biblical historical narratives as a cryptic mixture of their own praise of God and God's reign with that of the heavenly spirits before the throne of God (*merkaba* esotericism or mysticism of the divine throne).

In the Qumran writings we have the oldest witnesses to the beginning of a new regulation of the festal Sabbath and daily life of prayer in contrast to the biblical models. The secessionists of Qumran modeled their community life on a practice of prayer divorced from the Temple and its sacrifices. According to their ideas, their piety and way of life were not only equal, but superior in value to the (previous!) divinely pleasing sacrifices in the Temple.

"When these become members of the Community in Israel according to all these rules, they shall establish the spirit of holiness according to everlasting truth. They shall atone (*le-kapper*) for the guilty rebellion and for the sins of unfaithfulness that they may obtain lovingkindness for the land, without the flesh of holocausts and the fat of sacrifice. The oblation of the lips shall be as an acceptable fragrance of righteousness, and perfection of way as a delectable free-will offering" (1 QS 9. 3-5).

The "oblation of the lips," that is, the community's prayer, was thus thought by the people of Qumran, in light of the fact that the Temple had been polluted and desecrated, to be the only way in which Israel could fulfill its obligations to its God. It was pleasing to God and could therefore take the place of the Temple cult, and consequently also of the biblical forms of prayer. This new idea of prayer could be consolidated in Qumran because the people there were able also to interpret themselves, in contrast to Jerusalem and the Temple, by means of strong liturgical-ideological conceptions. They alone were members of the covenant. As the "people of God's redemption" they were also contrasted with the nations who were condemned to destruction (1 QM 14. 5) and were therefore particularly predestined to a grateful praise of God. As important as their consciousness of redemption and covenant was their conviction that the earthly liturgy of prayer was in harmony with heavenly worship. Biblical imagery (especially Isa 6:1-3; Ezek 1, 8, and others) gave birth to new ideas in the Qumran community. The hymns of the Sabbath sacrifice (4 Q Shir-Shab; but also 1 QH 3. 19-23, and others) are typical. According to 4 Q 400/2, lines 1–8, the people of Qumran joined in the song of the heavenly hosts:

". . . praising your wondrous glory among the divine rulers of knowledge and the praiseworthiness of your reign among the most holy. They are worshipped in all the tents of God, and they are fearful to human designs, a wonder surpassing the divine and the human. They proclaim the majesty of his reign according to their knowledge. They exalt his glory above all the heavens of his reign. . . . But how shall we take our place among them, and how will our priesthood abide in their dwellings? And how can our holiness be compared to their all-surpassing goodness? And what is the sacrifice of the words of our dust in comparison to the knowledge of the highest divinities? . . . We will exalt the God of knowledge!"[2]

[2] See also the text and English translation in Carol Newsom, *Songs of the Sabbath Sacrifice: A Critical Edition* (Atlanta: Scholars Press, 1985) 110–17.

What is happening here is praise of the "God of the glory of his reign," as practiced on the Sabbath by the heavenly spirits (who were adorned with divine epithets), and the Sabbath community of the Qumran priests is joining in this heavenly song of praise. The election of the Qumran priests is thus expressed in mystery when their praise of God is incorporated in that of the angels. The Sabbath is fully realized in a communion of earth and heaven, and it is only the harmony of the two dissimilar communities that yields an adequate praise of God and of the glory of God's reign. The earthly community in isolation cannot achieve a worthy Sabbath praise of God, even though it knows in faith that it is more beloved by God than the angels; this is not only because it is sinful, but also because—in contrast to the lofty spirits of heaven—it has no view of the throne of God and the glory of God's power. The question: "But how shall we take our place among them?" is the humble confession of the community that has been chosen to participate in the heavenly liturgy.

Divine worship thus means being adopted into the heavenly service of worship, the high point of which, according to early Jewish (and rabbinic-esoteric) "throne of God mysticism" was the *trisagion* (*kedusha, sanctus*; cf. Isa 6:3). When the heavenly attendants at the throne of God cry out this threefold "holy," together with the human community, the Eternal One bows down to the angels and humans; this is an epiphany of God and the "kingdom of heaven" becomes a reality also amidst the "people of God's favor" (cf. Luke 2:14). This earthly-heavenly service of worship begins, for angels and humans, as a mutual and harmonious calling on God the three-times holy. This was not yet explicitly stated in Qumran itself.

The most solemn expression of this grandiose conception of divine worship is found in Revelation 4, an apocalyptic chapter that bears no traces of Christian influence. The one seated on the throne (4:2) is addressed with the threefold cry of holy (Isa 6:3; Rev 4:8). The twenty-four elders are the representatives of the cult of Israel. They join the heavenly creatures around the throne in praising God and God's reign: "You are worthy, our Lord and God, to receive glory and honor and power, for you created all things, and by your will they existed and were created" (Rev 4:11). This doxology emulates, among other passages, Exodus ·15:18, an old biblical liturgical text that was interpreted in early and rabbinic Judaism as foundational for the liturgy. The service of worship was said to be, in its first action, a doxological calling on God as king: "The eternal one will (or shall) be king forever and ever." In addition, the response of the people ("the great Amen") has influenced the cultic rite in the Temple as reflected in Revelation 4:11: "Blessed be the name of the glory of his kingdom forever and ever" (mYom 3.8; 4.1-2; 6.2: *barukh schem, kevôd malkhûtô, le-'ôlam wa-'ed*).

We may suppose that this response of the people in the Temple courts was not only intended as an affirmation of the prayers and cultic actions of the priests, but also an expression of the people's desire to be incorporated into the earthly-heavenly worshipping community.[3] Not only in Qumran and the New Testament do we find traces of this heavenly-earthly conception of worship, but also in the apocalyptic Book of Enoch (*1 Enoch* 61:9-11), in the apostolic fathers (*1 Clem* 34.6; Ign Eph 4.2), and among the rabbis (bHag 11b–16a, and frequently elsewhere).

Thus in its earlier forms Jewish worship of God is praise of God by a community devoted to God and God's kingdom, a praise that calls out to God and acknowledges the communion of heaven and earth. This praise of God the ruler emerges from the internal identity of the community. Liberated from all political and social restrictions, the praying community is aware of the invisible link, surpassing all earthly limits, between God and God's chosen creatures. This communion is an expression of the covenant between God and the praying people, which is accepted in faith. Thus the worship service is a *memoria*, a memory-made-present of the God who is faithful to the covenant, who turns graciously and in dialogue to God's heavenly and earthly creation, but especially to the people who are God's own.

---

[3] On this whole subject, cf. David Flusser, "Sanctus und Gloria," in his *Entdeckungen im Neuen Testament* (Neukirchen-Vluyn, 1987) 1:226–44; *idem*, "Jüdische Wurzeln des liturgischen Trishagion," 1:245–52.

2. *The Horizontal Type of Worship*

The first example that offers itself is the "hallel" of Ben Sira (ca. 180 B.C.E.): Sirach 51:12a-o. This liturgical song in alternating strophes can probably be traced to the third century B.C.E.; it is a secondary addition to the Book of Sirach. Formally, Ben Sira's "hallel" imitates the hallel-psalm 136. In the introduction, the praying community looks up to the God of glory (vertical component). Then, in the body of the prayer, there is a somewhat confused expression of grateful memory of the past, the introduction of reflections on the present, and future hopes. The central part is therefore primarily horizontal in its direction. The text reads:

a) Give thanks to the Lord, for he is good,
   for his mercy endures forever;
b) Give thanks to the God of praises,
   for his mercy endures forever;
c) Give thanks to the one who formed all things,
   for his mercy endures forever;
d) Give thanks to the guardian of Israel,
   for his mercy endures forever;
e) Give thanks to the redeemer of Israel,
   for his mercy endures forever;
f) Give thanks to the one who gathers the dispersed of Israel,
   for his mercy endures forever;
g) Give thanks to the one who rebuilt his city and his
   sanctuary,
   for his mercy endures forever;
h) Give thanks to the one who makes a horn to sprout for
   the house of David,
   for his mercy endures forever;
i) Give thanks to the one who has chosen the sons of Zadok
   to be priests,
   for his mercy endures forever;
j) Give thanks to the one who has chosen Zion,
   for his mercy endures forever;
k) Give thanks to the shield of Israel,
   for his mercy endures forever;
l) Give thanks to the rock of Israel,
   for his mercy endures forever;
m) Give thanks to the mighty one of Jacob,
   for his mercy endures forever;

n) Give thanks to the King of the kings of kings,
    for his mercy endures forever;
o) He has raised up a horn for his people,
    praise for all his loyal ones,
    for the children of Israel, the people close to him.
    Alleuia!

This liturgical "hallel" may have its *Sitz im Leben* in the Passover festival. Much like the "leaflet," probably also pre-Christian, found in Targum Neophyti 1 on Genesis 12:42, it suggests the four items that make up the Passover feast: (1) the creation of the world ("the one who formed all things": c); (2) God's saving deeds for the ancestors (k–m); (3) deliverance from Egypt (d–e); (4) messianic redemption (f–h, o). There are a number of echoes of the songs of rejoicing (for Passover): Psalms 118; 136; 147, as well as prophetic images of hope, e.g., Isaiah 11:12; 56:8.

There is in Judaism no Jewish liturgical Sabbath or festival ceremony with only *one* object; there are always *several* items of content touching past, present, and future. Nowadays in interpretations of Passover there is often a one-sided emphasis: it is said that this feast is devoted solely to the celebration of Israel's liberation and rescue from Egypt; that it is a *zikkaron*, a *memoria*, a recollection of the Exodus. This kind of festival exclusivism was not accurate for pre-Christian or rabbinic times. All Jewish feasts, holidays and Sabbaths, apparently from the beginning, included several memorials. They are liturgical collations of the heavenly with the earthly and of faith experiences extending over a long period of time.

But let us for the moment focus on the Passover feast. Its mysteries were listed in Targum Neophyti on Exodus 12:42, mentioned above. This is an ancient fragment of a Targum from a period shortly before Christ. Its original function was probably to remind Jews celebrating Passover of the things that were to be commemorated at the feast. Form-critically, we could call it a liturgical leaflet or "memo." The text reads:

"That was a night of vigil for the Lord, to bring them out
of the land of Egypt (Exod 12:42).
"It is *a night of vigil*. It is devoted to liberation in the name
of the Eternal One, as at the time of the exodus of the chil-

dren of Israel who were delivered from the land of Egypt.
But there are *four nights* that are written in the book of
memorials:

"*The first night:* When the Eternal One was revealed to the
world to create it. The earth was a formless void. Darkness
covered the face of the deep. The word of the Eternal One
was the light. It illuminated and named this night the first
night.

"*The second night:* When the Eternal One was revealed to
Abraham, when he was a hundred years old and his wife
Sarah was ninety. That the Scripture might be fulfilled: 'See,
Abraham is a hundred years old, and shall he be able to be-
get a child? And his wife Sarah is ninety, and shall she be
able to bear a child?' (Gen 17:17). Isaac was thirty-seven years
old when he sacrificed himself on the altar. The heavens
descended and came down. Isaac saw their glory, and because of it his eyes were darkened. And he called this night
the second night.

"*The third night:* When the Lord was revealed to the Egyp-
tians at midnight. His hand killed the firstborn of Egypt, and
his right hand protected the firstborn of Israel. That the Scripture might be fulfilled: 'Israel is my firstborn son' (Exod 4:22).
And he called this night the third night.

"*The fourth night:* When the world shall reach its consum-
mation and be delivered. The iron chains will be broken. The
generations of evil will be swept away. Moses will come forth
from the midst of the desert and the King Messiah from the
heart of the heavens. They will stand on the pinnacle of a
cloud (or: host). His word will stand between them. Both
of them will proceed as one.

"This is *the night of Passover* in the name of the Eternal One,
the night of watching. And it is for the liberation of all generations of Israel."[4]

There are thus four items contained in the Passover feast:
(1) creation of the world; (2) Abraham's readiness to sacrifice
his son Isaac, and the "yes" to this act of obedience by Isaac

[4] The Aramaic text was edited by Alejandro Diez Macho, *Neophyti 1,
Targum Palestinense MS de la Biblioteca Vaticana* (Madrid, 1970) 2:77–79; cf.
Roger LeDéaut, *La Nuit Pascale* (Rome: Pontifical Biblical Institute, 1963).
See also B. Barry Levy, *Targum Neophyti 1. A Textual Study.* 2 vols. Studies
in Judaism (New York: University Press of America, 1986, 1987).

in his maturity: In Jewish tradition the heroic act of faith on the part of Abraham and Isaac, drawn from Genesis 22, is called *akeda* (= the binding or chaining of Isaac, referring to Gen 22:9); (3) The liberation of the Israelites from slavery in Egypt; (4) The future messianic liberation. All four are given the same value, but at the beginning and end of this liturgical leaflet it is emphasized that the four nights—that is, the four festal mysteries—are summed up in the *one* night of liberation from Egypt. Hence the Exodus event constitutes the unifying center of the manifold memorials in the Passover feast.

Alongside these four principal events, the rabbinic and Jewish liturgical tradition acknowledges still other items of content for Passover: the destruction of Sodom and Gomorrah, an event in which the idolatrous worship of sun and moon was also destroyed (BerR 50.12); the promise, birth, and blessing of Isaac (BerR 48.12; bRHSh 10b-11a; TJ on Gen 27:6).[5] In the evening prayer for the first day of Passover, in a kind of litany, there is an unsystematic listing of all the things that were celebrated at Passover in times past; it is said many times that all this is true today as once in the exodus from Egypt: the eating of the paschal lamb, the miracles at the departure and at the Red Sea, the suffering of the faithful, the killing of the firstborn of Egypt, the giving of the law at Mount Sinai, God's judgment on sinners, the return of the redeemed to Zion, and so on.[6]

Thus at Passover both past and future are brought into the present. Hence Passover is a feast of *memoria*, of *zikkaron*, of remembrance, memorial, and hope. What is decisive is that God is implored to make the past events of salvation graciously present and effective and to prefigure future saving events in the festival community by causing them to illuminate the celebrants. This inclusion of all possible elements can be observed in other Jewish festivals as well. It shows that the celebration of faith in Judaism is not isolationist, but always

---

[5] Cf. Clemens Thoma and Simon Lauer, eds., *Die Gleichnisse der Rabbinen. Zweiter Teil: Von der Erschaffung der Welt bis zum Tod Abrahams: Bereschit Rabba 1-63*. Judaica et Christiana 13 (Berne, 1991) 295-96.

[6] Cf. Selig Bamberger, ed., *Gebetbuch für das Pesachfest* 1 (Basel, 1943) 15.

echoes all the saving acts of God to the greatest extent possible. Passover is thus, in Jewish tradition, "the feast of feasts," but that is nothing unusual; the same can be said of Rosh Hashanah, of Yom Kippur, of the Feast of Weeks (Pentecost), and so on.

How this light from the past enters the consciousness of the celebrants is clear from the Passover *haggada*:

"In every age Jews are obliged to regard themselves as if they themselves had come out of Egypt. For it says: 'You shall tell your child on that day, "It is because of what the Lord did for me when I came out of Egypt" ' (Exod 13:8). Therefore are we bound to give thanks, to praise, to glorify, to honor, to exalt, to extol, and to bless the one who wrought all these wonders for our ancestors and for us. He brought us out from bondage to freedom, . . . so let us say before him the *Hallelujah*" (mPes 10.5).

God, for whom there are no restrictions of time or space, is asked to lead the celebrants into the past time of salvation, or else to make that past salvation present, so that those celebrating today may exhibit the gifts and characteristics of liberated persons just as the Israelites did. The awareness in faith that the liberating God is really at work in the Passover of today, in renewing the Passover blessings, creates a halleluja-mood in the community of tradition and faith.

The most important *memoria* figure in Judaism is Abraham. Rabbinic Judaism's interpretation of his obedience in faith in the "binding of Isaac" (Gen 22) is probably the best illustration of the intensity and extent of memorial piety. After the description of how God relieved Abraham of the terrible task of slaughtering his son, Targum Neophyti 1 says, apropos of Genesis 22:14:

"Abraham sank down in adoration and called on the name of the word of the Lord and uttered a prayer for mercy: 'Before you, O Lord, all things are open, and all is known to you. There was no division in my heart in all the time before now, because you said to me that I should sacrifice my son Isaac, and make him to be dust and ashes before you. Instead, I arose early and in haste and was glad and ready to fulfill your word, and so I obeyed your commandment. And now, when my children are in danger, they should remember the binding (*akeda*,

Gen 22:9) of their ancestor Isaac. Listen, then, to the voice of their prayer, answer them and rescue them from danger . . ." (similarly BerR 56.10 on Gen 22:14).

In texts like these we encounter that common "metal" to which Franz Rosenzweig referred, which is the life and nourishment of Christian sacramental worship as well. In the *akeda*, the *memoria* receives an explicit utterance.

But the praying community cannot exhaust its prayer in the praise of God and God's reign. It also has desires, needs, and difficulties. It is characteristic of Jewish worship that the petitions are very seldom expressed without being surrounded by divine praise. We may illustrate this in the eighth prayer of the Eighteen Benedictions:

"Heal us, O Lord, and we shall be healed; save us, and we shall be saved. . . . Blessed art thou, O Lord, who heals the sick of thy people Israel."

The praise of God penetrates the very heart of the prayer: if you heal us, we are truly healed; if you redeem us, we are truly redeemed; you are to be praised for your perfect deeds! Similarly artistic combinations of praise and petition are found in a great many Jewish liturgical passages. On the vigil of Yom Kippur there are some psychologically masterful transitions and pauses between the praise of God, the enumeration of sins, and prayers for forgiveness. One of these petitions reads: "For all these [sins], O God of forgiveness, forgive us, grant us remission (*we'al kullam selach lanû, mechal lanû, kapper lanû*). This is repeated throughout the litany, whenever the listing of sins threatens to become flat or the praise of God monotonous.[7]

The liturgical politeness which requires that one not simply blurt out one's wishes is found also in Christian liturgy, in the prayers of the Church. It is really too bad that teachers of private prayer so seldom remind people that it is proper to utter a reminder of God's saving deeds and greatness before asking for something.[8]

---

[7] Cf. Daniel Goldschmidt, ed., *Mahazor la-yamim ha-nora'im* . . . (Jerusalem: Koren [1970]) 730.

[8] Cf. Hans Henrix, ed., *Jüdische Liturgie: Geschichte, Struktur, Wesen,* QD 86 (Freiburg: Herder, 1979) especially 53–55.

II. Worship of God as Carrying Out the Covenant

Our interest now is to give some theological content to this train of thought. *Memoria* means covenant, renewal of covenant, celebration of covenant, carrying out of covenant. We will expound this by using a passage from the *kedusha* to the Mussaf on the Sabbath and the major feasts in an Ashkenazi expansion:

" 'Hear, O Israel, the Lord is our God, the Lord alone' (Deut 6:4). He is our king, our redeemer, our counselor. And he will redeem us a second time, he will in his mercy make us known in the eyes of all living things. He will then say: 'See, I have redeemed you at the end as in the beginning, that I may be your God.' "[9]

The principal meaning of this *beraka* can be deduced from its conclusion. It is a part of the covenant formula in the Hebrew Bible, the most extensive form of which is found in Deuteronomy 26:16-19:

> This very day the Lord your God is commanding you to observe these statutes and ordinances; so observe them diligently with all your heart and with all your soul. Today you have obtained the Lord's agreement: to be your God; and for you to walk in his ways, ... Today the Lord has obtained your agreement: to be his treasured people (*'am segullah*), . . . and to keep his commandments; for him to set you high above all nations that he has made, in praise and in fame and in honor; and for you to be a people holy (*'am kadôsh*) to the Lord your God, as he promised.

This statement, that God and God's people have a special mutual relationship, a partnership, appears very frequently in the Torah (Gen 17:7, [Abraham]); Lev 11:45; 22:33; 25:38; 26:45; Num 15:41; Deut 7:6; 14:2, and elsewhere). Jewish worship is also a covenant event, a renewal of covenant and an anticipation of covenant. The *memoria* expresses this divine-human event. It is an intersection toward which past mutual experiences of God and humanity run and from which tracks are laid that lead into a divine-human future of partnership.

[9] Cf. Selig Bamberger, ed., *Gebetbuch für den Versöhnungstag* (Basel, 1953) 191.

This awareness of the covenant event that is continually represented in worship is connected with a fundamental Jewish self-concept. The Jewish people is a nation redeemed countless times. The last redemption and the last confirmation of its redemption, of its nearness to God in dialogue (cf. Ben Sira's *hallel*, "the people close to him") will be revealed before the eyes of all nations.

According to Martin Buber (1878–1965) it "can be proved" that "there is scarcely any Christian sacrament that does not have a sacramental or quasi-sacramental Jewish model." In the sacrament "the covenant of the Absolute with the concrete" is achieved. "Where the covenant appears it is like a mirror image of something invisible; where the covenant appears it is like a hand within a hand."[10] In Buber's thinking, and in a considerable part of Jewish tradition, the idea of covenant must stand as a background to the question of *memoria*. This is summarized in a rabbinic blessing: "Blessed is He who remembers the Covenant, . . . Who is faithful with his Covenant and fulfils his word" (bBer 59a). The idea of the coherence of creation and human history is related to this. The rabbis said, for example: "Of all that the Holy One, blessed be He, has created in His world, He did not create a single thing without pupose (*le battala*)" (bShab 77b). Everything is incorporated in the covenant and thereby arrives at its originally intended place. The human task is keeping this covenant continually alive and renewing it through the celebrations of faith and the daily fulfillment of the commandments.

It is frequently emphasized that liturgy, as a covenant event or as a sacramental event, also includes *hope for the future end*. Confidence in God is only complete when the future God has prepared is believed in, hoped in, and accepted into human hearts as the confluence of all that is past and present. A midrash on Genesis 22:5 (BerR 56.2) expresses it this way:

> "And I and the lad will go yonder, and we will worship, and we will come back to you" (Gen 22:5). . . . Rabbi Isaac said: Everything happened as a reward for worshipping (*hak-*

[10] Martin Buber, "Sinnbildliche und Sakramentale Existenz im Judentum," in *Eranos-Jahrbuch* (Zürich, 1943) 2:352–59.

kol bizkhût hishtahawaya). Abraham returned in peace from Mount Moriah only as a reward for worshipping. . . . Israel was redeemed only as a reward for worshipping: "And the people believed . . . then they bowed their heads and worshipped" (Exod 4:31). The Torah was given only as a reward for worshipping: "And worship ye afar off" (Exod 24:1). Hannah was remembered only as a reward for worshipping: "And she worshipped before the Lord" (1 Sam 1:10). The exiles will be reassembled only as a reward for worshipping: "And it shall come to pass in that day, that a great horn shall be blown; and they shall come that were lost . . . and that were dispersed . . . and they shall worship the Lord in the holy mountain at Jerusalem" (Isa 27:13). The Temple was built only as a reward for worshipping: "Exalt ye the Lord our God, and worship at His holy hill" (Ps 99:9). The dead will come to life again as a reward for worshipping (*ham-metîm chayîm*): "O come, let us worship and bend the knee, let us kneel before the Lord our Maker!" (Ps 95:6).

Liturgical prayer has an irrevocable direction toward the future. It is only fulfilled in believing acceptance of the future. The conviction of redemption and the hope for still greater salvation that is connected with it has further effects in the Jewish liturgy: for example, in the so-called Sephardic version of the Mussaf prayer (18th c.) on the Sabbath: "See, I have redeemed you (*ga'alti*) for perfection, I, the Lord."

III. Conclusions

(1) Jewish people in the modern and post-modern periods, like Christians, have become more matter-of-fact when it comes to giving meaning to their worship. Divine worship is an assembly of the community, and therefore has a social function. Community within the religious sphere creates its own cohesion. This does not represent any trivialization of older ideas of worship, for the notion of covenant also has its place in this conception. There would only be banalization if the worship service declined into individuals' unloading of things that weigh on their souls, without any connection to the community, or if it represented nothing more than a desire for edifi-

cation that could be satisfied by a good performance of the Mozart Requiem.·

(2) In light of Israel's faith, Jesus' words, "do this in memory of me" (1 Cor 11:24; Luke 22:19) should be interpreted in prayer as follows: "Lord, God of our ancestors, we praise you for what you have done for Jesus Christ and what Jesus Christ has done for us. Renew the event of the Supper in our days and in our community. Let it be present for us as a saving event that is past and still to come. Make us vessels of this event. Praise to you who remember your covenant, who are true to your covenant and to your words (cf. Ber. 59a). Praise to you who have created nothing without purpose (bShab. 87a). Praise to you who have made the breaking of bread and drinking the cup to be signs of your covenant in Jesus Christ."

In contrast to this, what we sometimes hear from ministers of the Eucharist after the words of institution is sheer platitude. "When you do this, remember me." *Memoria* is not merely thinking of Christ and his death agonies, but praise for God's work in Christ in the past, the present, and the future, and through the Christ of the past, present, and future. It is also an expression of confidence that every redemption given and to be given by God throws a beam of light into the present of the liturgical community.

(3) A study of the history of revelation and the anticipation of salvation in the future should be, in Christianity as it is in traditional Judaism, a fundamental component in all religious instruction and a part of every sermon. If we continue to insist too much on the logical and pedagogical question of how people can still have faith today and how those present at worship can be put in the right mood, and if in doing so we neglect the story of revelation and expectation, we dilute Christianity and will never escape from our plight. Here we may recall the Catholic celebration of the Easter Vigil, which has the same content as the Passover that Judaism has celebrated since a time before Christianity: creation of the world (First Reading), Abraham's faithful obedience (Second Reading), delivery from Egypt (Third Reading), and messianic expectation (Fourth Reading).

These four readings are material that is indispensable in our preparation for Easter. They should never be omitted from the

Easter Vigil (to make time for blessing Easter baskets or whatever)! The Easter Vigil presents the *memoria* of the whole history of faith in Israel and in the Church, from the creation of the world to the *eschaton*, in the course of which, according to Christian conviction, the "Christ of glory" (Jas 2:1) will appear, the one whom we celebrate as the Redeemer who has already come. Here the vertical type of worship also plays its part: the kingdom of heaven whose first representative is the exalted Lord (cf. Heb 1) descends to the community of those celebrating, as once it came down to the shepherds at Bethlehem (Luke 2:8-20).

Philipp Schäfer

3. Eucharist: Memorial of the Death and Resurrection of Jesus

I. Introduction: Historical Notes

In the texts he composed for the feast of Corpus Christi and for the Eucharist, Thomas Aquinas (d. 1274) both adhered to the traditions of the ancient Church and strongly emphasized the real presence of Christ in the Eucharist and the adoration of the sacrament.[1] In the antiphon for the *Magnificat* at second vespers of Corpus Christi he writes: "How holy this feast in which Christ is our food; his passion is recalled; grace fills our hearts; and we receive a pledge of the glory to come, alleluia."[2] In this antiphon, very much in harmony with his theology and his description of the Eucharist, Thomas interprets the Eucharist as the memorial of Christ's passion. By "passio," that is, "passion," he means not only Jesus' death, but his resurrection as well. In the language of theology and liturgy, "passio" describes Jesus Christ's progress through cross and resurrection to the Father. On the other hand, Thomas sees that this memorial transmits and mediates grace to people now

[1] These texts include: *Adoro te devote; Pange lingua; Lauda Sion salvatorem.*

[2] "O sacrum convivium, in quo Christus sumitur: recolitur memoria passionis eius, mens impletur gratia, et futurae gloriae nobis pignus datur, alleluia" (Liturgia horarum, Solemnitas Sanctissimi Corporis et Sanguinis Christi. Ad II Vesperas, Ad Magnificat antiphona). *ICEL* translation, 1975.

and furnishes a pledge of future glory. The Eucharist is a memorial that is effective in the present, and it is also a promise for the future.

Thomas formulates here for the Eucharist the idea that is important for him in his doctrine of the sacraments. The sacraments are memorial or recollection of Christ's death and resurrection; they produce grace now and are a promise for the future. Sacraments are signs of memory, signs of a present event of grace, and signs of promise.[3] It is true that in his description of the Eucharist in the third part of his *Summa*, Thomas does not say explicitly that the Eucharist is a memorial of the death and resurrection of Christ. He primarily addresses questions regarding the real presence of Christ, the words of institution, and the ritual. In treating these questions, Thomas repeatedly argues that the Eucharist is the memorial of the Lord's passion. It can be called a sacrifice because it memorializes the suffering that is the true sacrifice.[4] The sacrament is celebrated in bread and wine, the body and blood of Christ, because it is a memorial of Christ's passion.[5] He describes its effects in terms of what the sacrament represents, and that is the passion of Christ.[6] Thomas clearly presumes that the Eucharist is a memorial of the death and resurrection of Jesus, but he neither probes that idea nor describes it in more detail. The questions that he directly addresses relate to other topics. The Eucharist is, for Thomas, quite obviously a memorial of the passion of Christ that makes that passion present. This he

[3] "Unde sacramentum est et signum rememorativum eius quod praecessit, scilicet passionis Christi; et demonstrativum eius quod in nobis efficitur per Christi passionem, scilicet gratiae; et prognosticum, idest praenuntiativum, futurae gloriae" (*Summa Theologiae* III, 60, 3 (with reference to Alexander of Hales, *Summa Theologiae* p. 4 q. 1 m. 1).

[4] "Inquantum scilicet est commemorativum Dominicae passionis, quae fuit verum sacrificium" (*S.T.* III, 73, 4c).

[5] "Quod est memoriale Dominicae passionis, seorsum sumitur panis ut sacramentum corporis, et vinum ut sacramentum sanguinis" (*S.T.* III, 74, 1; cf. *S.T.* III, 76, 2 ad 1).

[6] "Secundo consideratur ex eo quod per hoc sacramentum repraesentatur, quod est passio Christi, sicut supra dictum est. Et ideo effectum quem passio Christi fecit in mundo, hoc sacramentum facit in homine" (*S.T.* III, 79, 1; cf. 74, 1; 76, 2 ad 1).

repeatedly presumes in his argument,[7] but he does not deal with it explicitly.

In interpretations of Thomas' theology since the sixteenth century, this idea was overlooked and was no longer addressed. Late medieval theology was more interested in questions of sacrifice and in attempting to demonstrate why it makes sense to celebrate the Eucharist for the dead. The Eucharist is understood as Mass, as a sacrifice for the living and the dead.

The Catholic apologists found it very difficult to show how the sacrifice of the Mass was connected with Christ's sacrifice on the cross. Johannes Eck (1486–1543) distinguished the unbloody offering of the body and blood of Christ from the sacrifice of the cross. He called the Mass an unbloody offering and another sacrifice.[8] The Franciscan Kaspar Schatzgeyer (1464–1527), and the learned bishop of Chiemsee, Berthold Pürstinger (1465–1543) were able to use their knowledge of the apostolic fathers to show how the Eucharist was a making present of the sacrifice of the cross.[9]

The Council of Trent understood the sacrifice of the Mass as a representation or making present and a memorial of the sacrifice of the cross. The conciliar fathers pointed to the celebration of Passover as a memorial of the exodus from Egypt and said that Christ offers himself by the Church through the priest under visible signs, in a memorial of his departure from

---

[7] Cf. *S.T.* III, 73, 5, 6; 74, 1.

[8] Cf. Erwin Iserloh, "Johannes Eck," in: *Katholische Theologen der Reformationzeit* (Münster, 1984) 1: 68/69, with further bibliographical references at 71.

[9] Cf. Kaspar Schatzgeyer, *Schriften zur Verteidigung der Messe*, edited and introduced by Erwin Iserloh and Peter Fabisch, CCath 37 (Münster, 1984), 422 and frequently elsewhere; Erwin Iserloh, "Kaspar Schatzgeyer," in: *Katholische Theologen der Reformationszeit* (Münster, 1984) 1:60–63; Gerhard Marx, *Glaube, Werke und Sakramente im Dienste der Rechtfertigung in den Schriften von Berthold Pürstinger, Bischof von Chiemsee*, Erfurter Theologische Studien 45 (Leipzig, 1982); Karl Zöller, *Die Messopferlehre des Berthold von Chiemsee nach seiner "Tewtschen Theologey."* Dissertation (Freiburg, 1979); Philipp Schäfer, "Katholische Theologie im Zeitalter der Reformation," in: *Handbuch Bayer. Kirchengeschichte*, edited by Walter Brandmüller (in press).

this world to the Father, because he redeemed us by shedding his blood, freed us from the power of darkness, and led us into his kingdom.[10] According to Trent, the Eucharist was instituted as, and is, a sacrificial memorial of Jesus Christ's departure from this world to the Father.

Later theology has not, so far as I can see, addressed this point of view. The memorial character of the Eucharist, as well as the other sacraments, was rediscovered by Odo Casel (1886–1948) and the mystery theology he initiated.[11] Also significant were the various forms of the liturgical movement[12] and the reawakened interest in patristic theology that marked the first half of this century. Casel's mystery theology excited a lively controversy in which theologians from Münster including Gottlieb Söhngen, Michael Schmaus, and Otto Kuß participated. The heart of Casel's interest and intent have received increasing acceptance.

The fathers of Vatican Council II, who owed much to these movements, introduced the idea of the Eucharist as memorial celebration into the conciliar texts. The Eucharist is understood there as a making present of the death and victory of Christ, in thanksgiving for this unspeakably great gift.[13] Vatican II's

[10] "Nam celebrato veteri Pascha, quod in memoriam exitus de Aegypto multitudo filiorum Israel immolabat (Ex 12,1 ss), novum instituit Pascha, se ipsum ab Ecclesia per sacerdotes sub signis visibilibus immolandum in memoriam transitus sui ex hoc mundo ad Patrem, quando per sui sanguinis effusionem nos redemit 'eripuitque de potestate tenebrarum et in regnum suum transtulit' (Col 1, 13)." Concilium Tridentinum, Sessio 22, 17 Sept. 1562, Cap. 1 (DS 1741).

[11] Cf. Theodor Filthaut, *Die Kontroverse über die Mysterienlehre* (Münster, 1947); Burkhard Neunheuser, ed., *Opfer Christi und Opfer der Kirche. Die Lehre vom Messopfer als Mysteriengedächtnis in der Theologie der Gegenwart* (Düsseldorf, 1960); Arno Schilson, *Theologie als Sakramententheologie. Die Mysterientheologie Odo Casals* (Mainz, 1982); Angelus A. Häussling, "Bibliographie Odo Casel 1967–1985," *ALW* 28 (1986): 26–42; Salvatore Marsili, "Das Gedächtnis des Herrn in der Theologie der Gegenwart, besonders in der Schau Odo Casals," *ALW* 22 (1980) 9–29.

[12] Cf. Schilson, *Theologie,* 58–97 (bibliography).

[13] "Similiter quotiescumque dominicam cenam manducant, mortem Domini annuntiant donec veniat" (*SC* 6). Cf. Anton Hänggi, "Das Gedächtnis in der Liturgie—Neue Ansätze im Zweiten Vatikanischen Kon-

Constitution on the Liturgy explicitly calls the sacred mystery of the Eucharist a memorial celebration:

> At the Last Supper, on the night when He was betrayed, our Savior instituted the Eucharistic Sacrifice of His Body and Blood. He did this in order to perpetuate the sacrifice of the Cross throughout the centuries until He should come again, and so to entrust to His beloved spouse, the Church, a memorial of His death and resurrection: a sacrament of love, a sign of unity, a bond of charity, a paschal banquet in which Christ is consumed, the mind is filled with grace, and a pledge of future glory is given to us.[14]

II. The Institution of the Eucharist as a Memorial Celebration

When Christians celebrate the Eucharist, they do so in reference to Jesus' Last Supper. All four accounts of the supper in the New Testament are modeled on the Eucharistic meal as it was celebrated in the communities of the evangelists or those known to Paul. The account of the Last Supper therefore derived its form in large part from a liturgical celebration. Exegetes do not dispute this, but they clearly are interested in discovering within the accounts a memory of the event of the Last Supper itself. Thus the four reports describe the celebration of the Eucharist in the communities. All four refer to Jesus' meal with his disciples on the evening before his passion. The form of the Eucharistic celebration shows that it is clearly a memory of what Jesus did at that meal. Luke's and Paul's accounts mention Jesus' giving a command: "Do this in remembrance of me."[15] In Paul's description there is another formula that can be understood as more than a simple remark: "Do this, as often

---

zil," in: Karl Schmid, ed., *Gedächtnis, das Gemeinschaft stiftet* (Munich and Zürich, 1985) 108–24.

[14] "Ecclesiae dilectae Sponsae memoriale concederet Mortis et Resurrectionis suae . . . vinculum caritatis, convivium paschale, in quo Christus sumitur, mens impletur gratia et futurae gloriae nobis pignus datur" (*SC* 47). For the "vinculum caritatis," reference is made to Augustine, *In Ioannis Evangelium Tractatus* 26.6.13 (PL 35.1613); for the last words, see n. 2 above (although here the text follows the liturgical books current at the time of the council).

[15] Luke 22:19; 1 Cor 11:24 (at the breaking of bread).

as you drink it, in remembrance of me.''[16] Because the reports of the Last Supper are modeled on the community's celebration, their shape and form attests that the Church has obeyed the command to do this, and that it celebrated the Eucharist as a memorial of the Lord.

The New Testament clearly attests that the primitive community understood the Last Supper as the institution of the Eucharist and intended in its celebration to fulfill the Lord's command to do this in his memory. In primitive Christian understanding, or in the understanding of the New Testament writers, the Eucharist is a memorial celebration. It is a memorial of what Jesus did at the Last Supper. He gave the bread as his body that would be given up for many, and he gave the cup of wine as his blood that would be poured out for many. The content of the memorial is Jesus' surrender to the Father in suffering on the cross for human beings.

Exegetes have inquired about the context in which this memorial or ''anamnesis'' is to be understood. Reference has been made to Greek memorial banquets for the dead, but it was objected that the expression ''in remembrance'' (*eis anamnesin*) cannot be demonstrated in the context of Greek memorial meals. Reference is also made to the Old Testament and to Jewish cultic memorial formulae in the Passover feast (Exod 12:14).

The first three Gospels think it important to describe the Last Supper in the context of a Passover meal. They say explicitly that a Passover supper was prepared and that, during that meal, Jesus took bread and shared the cup. Karl Kertelge asserts that the Passover motif is more than a mere framing device adopted before the Markan redaction; it is the salvation-historical basis and origin of a new liberation realized in Jesus' death, but already demonstrated symbolically in the meal celebration that preceded it.[17] Johannes Betz states it this way:

[16] (At the sharing of the cup) 1 Cor 11:25 and its continuation: ''for as often as you eat this bread and drink this cup, you proclaim the Lord's death until he comes'' (v. 26).

[17] Cf. Karl Kertelge, ''Das Abendmahl Jesu im Markusevangelium,'' in: Josef Zmijewski and Ernst Nellessen, eds., *Begegnung mit dem Wort. FS Heinrich Zimmermann*, BBB 53 (Bonn, 1980) 67–80, at 69–70; Josef Ernst, *Das Evangelium nach Markus* (Regensburg, 1981) 422.

"Jesus takes up and gives content to the memory and expectation of God's saving acts. He makes the giving of his Eucharistic gifts a depiction of the new saving reality that will be constituted in his person and in his surrender to atoning death; he shows the new covenant and anticipates the completion of salvation in the *basileia*."[18]

The Passover meal itself is the memorial celebration of the great liberating act of God in delivering God's people from Egypt. In the description of the institution of the Passover meal in Exodus and Deuteronomy, it had already been emphasized that "this day shall be a day of remembrance for you. You shall celebrate it as a festival to the Lord!" (Exod 12:14). The day is to be remembered through all future generations. Deuteronomy emphasizes that in those days no leavened bread is to be eaten: "For seven days you shall eat unleavened bread with it—the bread of affliction— . . . so that all the days of your life you may remember the day of your departure from the land of Egypt" (16:3). In the Passover celebration itself the foods are specifically interpreted as those that the ancestors ate in Egypt. The head of the household emphasizes that God's liberating deed for Israel in Egypt is now a present reality, saying that the people once were slaves, but next year will be free.[19] The saving act is experienced in the celebration as present and effective. In this celebration, a Jewish slave is free.

If it was important for the evangelists to say that Jesus celebrated his Last Supper in the context of a Passover meal and commanded that it be done in his memory, they are also saying that, just as in the Passover meal God's liberating action on behalf of Israel in Egypt becomes present, so Jesus' self-surrender becomes present for believers who take part in this celebration. By eating and drinking, believers enter into community with Christ who gave himself up for them. It is not a communion with someone who is dead, but with the Living One, the exalted Lord. At the same time, they are incorporated into his surrender to the Father for the many and that surrender is effective for them as atonement and forgiveness of sins.

[18] Johannes Betz, "Eucharistie als zentrales Mysterium," *Mysterium Salutis* 4/2 (Einsiedeln, Zürich, and Cologne, 1973) 194.

[19] At this point, the names of contemporaries are mentioned.

In light of the New Testament, the Eucharist must be understood as a memorial celebration of the death and resurrection of the Lord. In fidelity to the biblical witness, the Eucharist can only be celebrated and interpreted, in the first instance, as a memorial of Christ and of his departure to the Father. All other statements about the Eucharist must harmonize with this understanding.

III. The Witness of the Eucharistic Prayers

1. The Eucharistic Prayers of the Early Church

Hippolytus of Rome has handed on a Eucharistic prayer from the period around 200 C.E. that has been incorporated into the second of the Eucharistic prayers now in use. This prayer thanks God through his beloved servant Jesus Christ, whom God has sent in the last days. In this thanksgiving the life of Jesus from birth to surrender on the cross is described with the utmost brevity. The thanksgiving is a memorial of what God has done through Jesus Christ, and it is a remembrance of Jesus Christ and his work, especially his surrender to the Father for the many. Thanks are given for Jesus in these words: "when he was betrayed to voluntary suffering that he might destroy death, and break the bonds of the devil, and tread down hell, and shine upon the righteous, and fix a term, and manifest the resurrection. . . ."

Then follows the account of the Last Supper. The next prayer begins with the words: "Remembering therefore his death and resurrection, we offer to you the bread and the cup, giving you thanks because you have held us worthy to stand before you and minister [as priests] to you."[20] Then comes the prayer that the Spirit may be sent upon the gifts. The speaker continues: ". . . grant to all those who receive the holy things (to receive) for the fullness of the Holy Spirit for the strength-

[20] Text in Bernard Botte, *La tradition apostolique de Saint Hippolyte, Essai de reconstitution* (Münster, 5th ed. 1989) 12ff. German translation in Philipp Schäfer, *Lebensquelle Eucharistie* (Regensburg, 1985) 90–91. English in R. C. D. Jasper and G. J. Cuming, *Prayers of the Eucharist: Early and Reformed* (New York, 3d rev. ed. 1987) 35. "Priests" here means all the baptized in their universal priesthood, their immediate access to God.

ening of faith in truth; that we may praise and glorify you through your child Jesus Christ.'' This is a prayer for the Holy Spirit, the gift of the Risen One, in confidence that that Spirit will be given as gift in the celebration of the Eucharist. The Risen One, as giver of that gift, is present. A memorial celebration is not merely a retrospect. What is remembered is present in it: the Lord who gave himself up for the many.[21]

In the Eucharistic prayer in the *Apostolic Constitutions*, the praise of God, the creator of heaven and earth and of humanity, is expanded; God's saving deeds for the ancestors are exalted and all this forms a transition to the Sanctus. After the Sanctus thanks are given for Christ, who was also active in the creation and in the saving deeds of the old covenant, and who became human to redeem us. The life and departure of Jesus are described in their saving effects. In the transition to the memorial of the Last Supper, the prayer says: ''Remembering therefore what he endured for us, we give you thanks, almighty God, not as we ought but as we are able, and we fulfill his command. For in the night he was betrayed. . . .''[22] Throughout this Eucharistic prayer God is addressed as Father, Son, and Spirit. In some Eucharistic prayers this is explicitly developed.[23] In all of them, God is thanked for the saving work done in Jesus Christ, and it is more or less clearly stated in these memorial thanksgivings that the saving reality created by God the Father through Jesus Christ is here present and effective in the Spirit.

The prayer of thanksgiving is always addressed to God the Father, to whom thanks are given in the Spirit through Christ (although the latter is not expressly stated). Only in the Spirit is the community able to call God Father.[24] These prayers are

[21] Traces of Eucharistic prayers are also found in other early Christian writings: the *Letter to Diognetus* (ca. 200) 7.1-2 and 9.2; the *Didache* 9, 10, and 14; Justin, *Apology* 1:65-67, and *Dialogue with Trypho* 41.1, 3; 117.1, 3.

[22] *Apostolic Constitutions* 8.12.35; Franz Xaver Funk, *Didascalia et Constitutiones Apostolorum* (Paderhorn, 1905) 1: 496-515, at 508, 16ff.; Anton Hänggi and Irmgard Pahl, *Prex Eucharistica* (Fribourg, 1968) 92; Jasper and Cuming, 110.

[23] ''Liturgy of the Twelve Apostles,'' in Hänggi and Pahl, 265ff. According to those authors, the examples could easily be multiplied.

[24] Cf. Rom 8:15; Gal 4:6.

thanksgiving brought to God the Father through Christ in the Spirit, thanks for God's actions for the salvation of human beings in the Son, our Lord Jesus Christ, who as the Risen One gives us his Spirit. This is the fundamental structure of all the Church's liturgical prayers.

In all Eucharistic prayers, the account of Jesus' Last Supper includes his command of institution: "Do this in remembrance of me." Some of the older prayers omit this brief command and substitute the words of promise found in Paul's First Letter to the Corinthians, formulating: "For as often as you eat this bread and drink this cup, you proclaim my death and confess my resurrection [and ascension] until I come."[25] Sometimes the formula of words is shorter: "When you do this, you will do it in memory of me."[26] This version appears primarily in the Egyptian region.

The Eucharist, according to these Eucharistic prayers, is a memorial thanksgiving for Christ's saving work, but also a sharing in the Christ who has gone to the Father. Johannes Betz concludes his study of the early Church's Eucharistic prayers with the words:

> Thus the anamnesis appears as a fundamental and essential feature of the entire *eucharistia*. The whole thing is a memorial of Christ's saving work. That idea is then intensified further in all the liturgies, in a pointed statement after the account of institution: "As we therefore remember the passion and resurrection. . . ."[27]

Thus it appears that the Eucharist is clearly to be understood and interpreted, on the basis of the Eucharistic prayers, as a memorial of Christ's passion. It is celebrated as a memorial of

[25] "Anaphora of Cyril of Alexandria," in Hänggi and Pahl, 137; see "The Liturgy of St. Mark: Final Form," Jasper and Cuming, p. 65, cf. also p. 56.

[26] "Anaphora Sanctorum patrum nostrorum apostolorum," in Hänggi and Pahl, 148; cf. "The Anaphora of the Twelve Apostles," Jasper and Cuming, 126.

[27] Johannes Betz, *Die Eucharistie in der Zeit der griechischen Väter 1/1. Die Actualpräsenz der Person und des Heilswerkes Jesu im Abendmahl nach der vorephesinischen griechischen Patristik* (Freiburg, 1954) 183.

the death and resurrection of the Lord. Death and resurrection summarize God's whole saving action in Christ.

2. *The Eucharistic Prayers in the Current Missal*

Let us now look at the four Eucharistic prayers in the missal now in use. After the unification of the liturgy in the post-Tridentine missal of Pope Pius V, there was only the one, Roman Eucharistic prayer, clearly set apart by the Sanctus and Preface from what had gone before. A number of prefaces were provided. These were related to the principal feasts, such as Christmas, Easter, and Pentecost, to weekdays, and to Masses for the dead. There was no freedom of choice. The missal that followed the liturgical reforms of Vatican II offers, in its German, English, and other vernacular editions, a rich selection of prefaces. However, theologians note that in the Prefaces for the feasts of saints or for particular occasions the thanksgiving for God's saving actions in Christ has been suppressed in favor of a thanksgiving for the effects of those saving acts in the Church and on behalf of believers.

The first, Roman Eucharistic prayer, initially attested in the fifth century, makes a sharp break at the *Sanctus* and interrupts the thanksgiving with petitions. The Roman Eucharistic prayer thus disrupts the structure of the prayers of the other Churches. It is not completely in accord with what is theologically required of a Eucharistic prayer.[28]

The second Eucharistic prayer is, as we have already indicated, modeled on the Eucharistic prayer in the *Apostolic Tradition* of Hippolytus. But in this second prayer the transition from memorial thanksgiving to memory of the Last Supper has been omitted. At that point it was again recalled that Jesus freely gave himself up to suffering for our salvation.[29]

Thus the second Eucharistic prayer, when it is used with a Preface that gives less attention to the saving event in Christ,

---

[28] Cf. Bruno Kleinheyer, *Erneuerung des Hochgebets* (Regensburg, 1969) 24ff.: "since the Roman canon shows significant deficiencies. . . ." (24).

[29] "when he was betrayed to voluntary suffering that he might destroy death, and break the bonds of the devil, and tread down hell, and shine upon the righteous, and fix a term, and manifest the resurrection, he took bread. . . ." (Botte, 90; Jasper and Cuming, 35).

is theologically deficient as a whole. However, the memorial is clearly described after the recollection of the institution at the Last Supper.

The third Eucharistic prayer recalls very briefly that God the Father, through the Son, in the power of the Holy Spirit has filled creation with life and grace and has gathered a people as God's own. Here, also, there is a clear statement after the account of the Last Supper that we are celebrating Christ's memorial.

The fourth Eucharistic prayer is very closely modeled on one type of Eucharistic prayer from the ancient Church. The Preface is designed more as praise of God. After the *Sanctus* there is a detailed remembrance of salvation history and of Jesus Christ and his actions. Even before the account of the Last Supper, it is said that the Spirit continues Jesus' work. Here also, after the account of institution, the celebration is described as a memorial of our redemption.

All four Eucharistic prayers include the command of institution and add to the words over the cup: "Do this in remembrance of me." There is thus a clear acknowledgment that the Church, in celebrating the Eucharist, is fulfilling Christ's command to commemorate his death and resurrection. The Eucharistic celebration is described, at its very center, as a memorial of the self-surrender of Jesus Christ in death and resurrection.

In the renewed liturgy an acclamation by the people has been inserted, for example: "We remember your death, O Lord, and we proclaim your resurrection until you come in glory."[30] This echoes the words of Paul in 1 Corinthians 11:26: "For as often as you eat this bread and drink the cup, you proclaim the Lord's death until he comes." The Eucharistic celebration is described as a proclamation of the death and resurrection of Jesus Christ. But proclamation is always remembering as well. Thus the Eucharistic celebration is understood as a remembrance of the death and resurrection of Jesus Christ.

[30] Here there is a shift in the address. The Eucharistic prayer is directed to God the Father; here it is Christ the Son who is addressed. With the exception of the third person acclamation "Christ has died; Christ is risen; Christ will come again," the other acclamations of the faithful suggested by the missal are also addressed to Christ.

Christian proclamation is not empty. When Christ's death and resurrection are proclaimed, they are present and effective. Proclamation is not simply an account of past events, but a promise of the reported and narrated saving reality for the hearers. This acclamation of the people witnesses to the memorial of the death and resurrection and acknowledges that this reality, Jesus Christ's self-surrender, is here present and effective. In addition, the acclamation shows that this reality exists here in history, in the time when, on the one hand, we can remember the saving event of Jesus Christ, and on the other hand, we await the return of Christ, the end of history.

All four Eucharistic prayers in the missal state very clearly, in accord with the account of institution and the acclamation of the people, that here we are celebrating the memorial of Jesus Christ, his death, his resurrection, and his ascension. With the description of this celebration as a memorial of Jesus Christ, the Son of the Father who is addressed, and of his saving acts, a transition is made to the petition for the Holy Spirit.

IV. The Patristic Witness

In the writings of the Church Fathers, we find early testimony to various features of the Eucharist. As early as the apostolic fathers there is attestation that the Eucharist brings believers into union with Christ and that in it they obtain a share in the body and blood of Christ.[31] According to Ignatius of Antioch, the Eucharist is "the flesh of our Savior Jesus Christ, which suffered for our sins and which, in his goodness, the Father has raised [from the dead]."[32]

The very name "eucharist" for the Lord's supper, which was generally accepted in early post-New Testament Christianity, tells us that the center of this celebration is thanksgiving. According to the Eucharistic prayers, the content of that thanksgiving, from the very beginning, was God's saving ac-

[31] Cf. Johannes Betz, *Eucharistie: in der Schrift und Patristik*, Handbuch der Dogmengeschichte [= HDG] 4/4a (Freiburg, 1979), 26ff.; Betz, *Eucharistie* 1/1, 158–59.

[32] Ign. *Smyrn.* 7.1 (translation by Cyril C. Richardson, *Early Christian Fathers* [New York, 1970]). Cf. Betz, *Eucharistie* 1/1, 184.

tion in Christ. The form of the thanksgiving is remembrance of Christ and his actions. The Eucharist is giving thanks for the Son of God who has come and who gave himself up for human beings in the cross and resurrection. It is thanksgiving that recalls God's saving deeds. Since in this celebration believers obtain a share in Christ and his work, what is remembered is effectively present.

According to Irenaeus, the Eucharist becomes the body and blood of Christ through the expression of thanks, a thanksgiving that is to be understood on the basis of the early Christian Eucharistic prayers. It is thanksgiving for the work of salvation in Jesus Christ.

For the Fathers, the memorial is very clearly expressed in their liturgical texts. Their theological efforts were devoted more to the questions of real presence and genuine sacrifice. They ordinarily explain the sacrifice on the basis of the memorial. The high priest assumed flesh and brought it to the Father as a sacrificial offering.[33] "The Savior's sacrifice, once offered, has perfected all things and is trustworthy because it always abides."[34] The sacrifice in the Church can only exist as the memorial of the sacrifice made once by the Savior. Cyril of Alexandria says: "The offering of this sacrifice is a memorial of the death and resurrection of Christ."[35] According to Gregory Nazianzen the Eucharist is an event in which the priest renews salvation and sacrifices the gifts of thanksgiving that are the image of the great mysteries.[36] The Fathers emphasize in different ways that in the Eucharist Christ is present as the one who acts and invites and offers sacrifice. The Syrians and Antiochenes speak very clearly of memorial. Theodore of Mopsuestia also explains the Eucharist in his catechesis for the newly baptized during Easter week. Although it is carried out in the forms of food and drink, it is a celebration of the

[33] Cf. Athanasius, *Contra Arianos Or.* 2.7 (PG 26.161 AB).

[34] Athanasius, *Contra Arianos Or.* 2.9 (PG 26.165 B). Cited from Betz, HDG 4/4a, 69.

[35] Cyril of Alexandria, *Glaph. in Ex.* 2 (PG 69.428 B); *In Jo 20,26* comm. 12 (PG 74.725 D); *Ad Nestorium epist.* 3.7 (ACO 1.1/1.37.22-25). From Betz, HDG 4/4a, 69.

[36] Cf. Betz, HDG 4/4a, 70.

memorial of the death of our Lord. Although we think that this is a memorial of his passion, because he says: "This is my body that was broken for you," it is clear that we perform the liturgy as a sacrifice. The Eucharist is a sacrifice. But it is not a new sacrifice, nor is it our own; it is a memorial of the true sacrifice of Christ, carried out in image and symbol.[37]

John Chrysostom sees the Eucharist as memorial, and in his descriptions of it returns again and again to Jesus' command of institution: "Do this in remembrance of me."[38] He tries to explain the Eucharist this way:

> The best way of preserving a good work is remembering it and continually giving thanks for it. Therefore also the noble mysteries that are full of abundant salvation and are carried out in every worship service are called eucharist (thanksgiving) because they are the memorial of many good works, they reflect God's providence, and they are a fundamental expression of thanksgiving.[39]

Christ himself is the one who invites and the one who acts. The priest is only there as a visible figure. Chrysostom speaks of the "memorial of his passion," the "symbol of his death."[40] The Eucharist is a sacrifice because in it Jesus' command "Do this in remembrance of me" is fulfilled and the memorial of Christ's passion is celebrated. Thus the same sacrifice is offered, "what we do is a memorial of the sacrifice."[41] Theodore of Mopsuestia attempts a kind of allegorical explanation of the Mass by connecting each part of the Eucharistic celebration with some event in the history of salvation.[42] Thus, for example, he sees the distribution of communion as a symbol of the resurrection. The breaking and sharing of the bread re-

[37] Cf. Theodore of Mopsuestia, *Katechetische Homilien* (Tonneau/Devreesse 15.15.485; similarly 15.21.497).

[38] Cf. Betz, *Eucharistie* 1/1, 189ff.

[39] John Chrysostom, *In Mt. Hom.* 25 (26).3 (PG 57.331); Betz, HDG 4/4a, 73.

[40] Cf. *In Mt. Hom.* 82 (83).1 (PG 58.739); cf. Betz, HDG 4/4a, 73.

[41] *In Hebr. Hom.* 17.3 (PG 63.131); cf. Betz, HDG 4/4a, 73.

[42] Cf. Theodore of Mopsuestia, *Katechetische Homilien* 15.20 (Tonneau/Devreesse, 497).

mind him of the death of Jesus and the appearances of the risen Christ.[43]

According to the Fathers, the saving action is not present in itself, but in the sacrament as its symbol. The symbol guarantees the objectivity of the commemorative real presence, the presence in memory. The Fathers see the presence of the past, unique event of salvation in the memorial celebration of the Eucharist as accomplished in symbol. The celebration of the Last Supper is symbolically a memorial of the passion of the Lord.

Clement of Alexandria calls the Last Supper the symbol of the Lord's passion and of his teaching.[44] Origen speaks of the bread of the Lord's supper as the *typikon kai symbolikon soma*, the body of Christ in image and symbol.[45] Eusebius of Caesarea says of the Eucharist: "We have received a memorial of this offering which we celebrate on a table by means of symbols of His Body and saving Blood."[46] The gifts can also be described as "the ineffable symbols of the Savior's passion."[47] "Bread and wine are called symbols of the body and blood of Christ to the extent that they represent to the senses the saving work of Jesus, the fate of his body and blood. In what happens to the elements that which once happened with and to the body and blood of Jesus is made present."[48]

It is the function of these symbols to accomplish the memorial action. They were handed over by Jesus together with the command: "Do this in remembrance of me."[49] According to Theodore of Mopsuestia, everything that has come to us through the death of Christ is made effective in us, in

[43] Cf. *ibid.* 16.16-17 (Tonneau/Devreesse 559).

[44] Cf. *Paidagogos* 1.6.49.3 (GCS 1.119.28–29). From Betz, *Eucharistie* 1/1, 218.

[45] Origen, *In Matth.* tom. 11.14 (GCS 10.59.8-9). From Betz, *Eucharistie* 1/1, 218.

[46] Eusebius of Caesarea, *Demonstratio evangelica* (*The Proof of the Gospel*) 1.10.29 (GCS 6.47.32-35); Betz, *Eucharistie* 1/1, 218.

[47] Eusebius, *Hist.eccl.* 10.3.3 (GCS 2.862.2-3).

[48] Betz, *Eucharistie* 1/1, 219.

[49] Cf. Betz, *Eucharistie* 1/1, 220, with reference to Pseudo-Chrysostom, *Hom.* 7 (PG 59, 751/52).

corresponding fashion, by the symbols of his death.[50] The original saving action of Jesus Christ is effected in us through being carried out in cultic form. These effects are accomplished by the symbols of the saving act. But Theodore distinguishes this from the presence of Christ in bread and wine. Jesus does not, in this instance, give us symbols, but himself.[51] Maximus the Confessor also sees the Eucharist in terms of memorial. It is true that he then interprets the Eucharist in terms of what happens within the souls of the participants, in the direction of a Eucharist in the soul.

It can therefore be said that in the Greek patristic literature the Eucharist was understood in terms of memorial. Individual statements and indications, especially regarding the question of sacrifice, are explained on the basis of the remembrance of the death and resurrection of Jesus Christ. The idea of memorial is connected with the present: the past, unique event of salvation is made present in the celebration of the Eucharist. It is true that the past saving event is not itself reproduced. It has not taken on an eternal mode of existence. Its presence is not absolute, but relative. The past event of salvation is symbolically present in the sacramental action. The Fathers do not give any more precise description of the presence of the saving act in the memorial celebration of the Eucharist. They speak of symbol, of image, and of type. But what is crucial is that they understand the Eucharist as a sacrifice, and interpret the real presence of the body and blood of Jesus Christ in the gifts of bread and wine in terms of a memorial of his passion and resurrection. For them, the Eucharist is primarily and fundamentally the fulfillment of Jesus' command: "Do this in remembrance of me."[52] In the West, the memorial character of the Eucharist was not so clearly emphasized. Augustine is acquainted with the idea. He says that Christians celebrate the memorial of Christ's sacrifice,[53] and calls the Eucharist the like-

[50] Cf. Betz, *Eucharistie* 1/1, 221.

[51] Cf. Betz, *Eucharistie* 1/1, 221. The words *eikon* (image), *homoioma* (likeness, similarity) and *typos* and *antitypos* are also frequently used. Cf. Betz, *ibid.* 223–24.

[52] Cf. Betz, *Eucharistie* 1/1, 241–42, and Betz, HDG 4/4a, 72ff.

[53] ". . . eiusdem sacrificii memoriam celebrant" (*Contra Faustum Man.* 20.18 [CSEL 25. 559]), quoted from Betz, HDG 4/4a, 154.

ness of that sacrifice. Christ has given us this celebration as a memorial of his passion.[54] Augustine regards the Eucharist primarily as a sacrifice, but he understands it as a sacrifice that commemorates the sacrifice of Jesus Christ.

At this point, then, the theology of the Eucharist as a memorial celebration of the passion of Jesus Christ is quite close to that of Thomas Aquinas. The Church's old Eucharistic tradition sees it as a memorial celebration of the Lord's death and resurrection. Ultimately, all other statements about the Eucharist are derived from this. As a memorial celebration of the supper that points forward to the death and resurrection of Jesus Christ, it makes the body and blood of Christ really present. As a memorial celebration of the unique self-surrender of the incarnate Son to the Father in his death on the cross, the Eucharist is a sacrifice. Some may find this conclusion overdrawn. But it is simply a fact that when both the Fathers and Thomas need arguments for understanding the Eucharist, they point to the memorial character of the celebration.

V. Newer Positions

1. The Discussion Before Vatican II

A lively controversy arose over Odo Casel's theology of mystery. Casel had rediscovered the memorial character of the Eucharist and of the whole pattern of Christian worship and showed that the mystery of the act of salvation is made present when its memorial is celebrated. Contemporary neoscholastic theologians could make nothing of this theology and opposed it. We will not go into that here. Other theologians gave further consideration to the question: how does the saving event become present?

For Odo Casel, "the Christian liturgy is the ritual carrying out of Christ's work of salvation in and through the *ecclesia* . . ., that is, the presence of the divine work of salvation under the veil of symbols."[55] It is his desire that this saving work

---

[54] ". . . qui se ipsum obtulit . . . et eius sacrificii similitudinem celebrandam in suae passionis memoriam commendavit" (Augustine, *De div. quaest.* 61.2 [CChr 44A, 122]).

[55] Odo Casel, "Mysteriengegenwart," in *JLW* 8:145 (from Betz, *Eucharistie* 1/1, 243).

should "really become present once more" and that Christians might achieve a genuine, mystical living and dying with Christ.[56]

This idea of the "presence of the divine work of salvation under the veil of symbols" was defended by some. It is true that Gottlieb Söhngen thought that Jesus' saving work was present and active in us not only in its fruits or effects, but that the saving deed itself is represented and made present. But he sees the presence of the saving work as existing in its effects. The saving effects of the action are the mystery that is present. The mystery of the past, unique act of salvation is made present. But he can also say that in the Mass the sacrifice of the cross "is represented as such with and for us."[57] Michael Schmaus and Hermann Kuhaupt[58] understand the presence of the saving work as taking the form of a memorial of the exalted Christ. For the risen Christ, the events of his life are not simply past, but are a living present. Whoever joins in community with Christ encounters those saving events that mark the existence of the transfigured Christ.

According to Johannes Betz the past, unique, historical saving work of Jesus Christ is present, but not in its historically conditioned circumstances. It is present in its core, in the act in which the whole of Jesus' saving work is gathered and concentrated at a single point: Jesus' self-surrender. Betz sees the past, unique event of salvation as appearing in a present event, the sacramental action. This saving work is not itself present in the Christian celebration, which has not taken on an eternal mode of being. The exalted Lord makes present the wealth of his person and his work, drawing human beings to himself and into his salvation. He does this in the word of proclama-

---

[56] *Ibid.*, 174.

[57] Gottlieb Söhngen, *Das sakramentale Wesen des Messopfers*, 1946, 14. "The sacrificial death of the Lord as an action is made present by the fact that it affects *us* in mystery, in that our action takes the same form as Christ's saving work and thus in this action the mystery of the cross is imitated in a mysterious way" (*Der Wesensaufbau des Mysteriums* [Bonn, 1938], 54–55, in Betz, *Eucharistie* 1/1, 254).

[58] Cf. Hermann Kuhaupt, *Die Feier der Eucharistie* 2 (Münster, 1950, 1951).

tion and in the symbolic action of the sacrament.[59] "Thus the unique, past, historical saving work of Jesus is present, not, of course, in its historically conditioned circumstances, but in its core, in the action in which the whole of the saving phenomenon of Jesus is gathered and concentrated to a single point. That is Jesus' free self-surrender to the Father, breathing ultimate meaning, in his bloody death on the cross, that is, the Passover mystery that removes the hypostatic union from time and implies the resurrection."[60]

The presence of Jesus Christ in the memorial celebration of the Eucharist is open to the future. With Jesus Christ's resurrection, the future has begun, and access to God is open. "The saving event occurred in time, but is not time-bound; therefore it does not pass away with time."[61]

The Italian Giraudo thinks that the Christ-event does not move and become present in the celebrating community, "but instead, in faith the community, by means of the liturgical celebration, makes itself present to the Christ-event—and this means the Christ-event that encompasses within itself past, present, and (eschatological) future."[62]

Lothar Lies, a student of Johannes Betz, attempts to extend the previous theology of memorial and making-present and to understand the sacrament, that is, the Eucharist as memorial celebration of the death and resurrection of the Lord, in terms of encounter.[63]

2. The Adoption of This Interest in Official Church Pronouncements

It is true that Vatican II adopted the interest in the idea of memorial. The Constitution on the Liturgy said that Christ had

[59] Cf. Johannes Betz, "Die Gegenwart der Heilstat Christi," in: Leo Scheffczyk, Werner Dettloff, and Richard Heinzmann, eds., *Wahrheit und Verkündigung. FS Michael Schmaus* (Paderborn, 1967), 1807–26, at 1821ff.

[60] *Ibid.*, 1821.

[61] Salvatore Marsili, "Das Gedächtnis des Herrn in der Theologie der Gegenwart, besonders in der Schau Odo Casels," *ALW* 22 (1980): 1–29, at 28.

[62] Cf. Hans Bernhard Meyer, "Odo Casels Idee der Mysteriengegenwart in neuer Sicht," *ALW* 28 (1986): 388–95, at 394.

[63] Lothar Lies, "Kultmysterium heute—Modell sakramentaler Begegnung. Rückschau und Vorschau auf Odo Casel," *ALW* 28 (1986) 2–21.

given the Mass to the Church as a memorial of his death and
resurrection.[64] In the *Institutio generalis Missalis Romani* of 1969,
we read: "The Lord's supper, that is, the Mass, is the assembly in which the people of God come together to celebrate . . .
the Lord's memorial." The second edition said: "in the Mass,
the Lord's supper, the people of God . . . is called together
to celebrate the Lord's memorial, the eucharistic sacrifice."[65]
Thus the idea of memorial was again suppressed in favor of
the idea of sacrifice. But the former point of view found increasing support in Church documents. In Pope Paul VI's instruction "on the cult of the eucharistic mystery," it is said
that in the Mass the memorial of the Paschal mystery is
celebrated. The true content of the memorial—and here what
is meant by "memorial" is the Eucharist—is said to be the death
and resurrection of the Lord.[66] In the decree on concelebration, in order to support the assertion that a multiplicity of
Masses does not reflect the uniqueness of the sacrifice of the
cross, it is pointed out that the Mass owes its character as sacrifice always and only to the fact that it is the memorial celebration of the bloody offering made once and for all by Christ on
the cross.[67]

Salvatore Marsili says of these texts: "It is a fact that
'memorial' and 'liturgy' have at the present time become inseparable concepts. Still more: memorial, as word and idea,
has become to a remarkable degree a characteristic mark of
post-conciliar liturgy."[68] In the liturgy "the concrete reality of
present salvation is celebrated by the memorial proper to it."[69]
Marsili thinks that Casel's interpretation has triumphed: "The
Mass is not a sacrifice in and of itself, but is identical with
Christ's death on the cross, to the extent that it is a memorial

[64] SC 47.

[65] "Ad memoriale Domini seu sacrificium eucharisticum celebran-
dum." Cf. Marsili, "Das Gedächtnis," 16.

[66] Cf. Instructio de cultu mysterii eucharistici, "Eucharisticum Mysterium," 25 May 1967, 10 (EDIL 908).

[67] Decree on concelebration, "Ecclesiae semper," 7 March 1965.

[68] Marsili, "Das Gedächtnis," 14.

[69] *Ibid.*, 15.

of it. Its sacrificial character therefore rests on its character as memorial. It is essentially sacrifice as memorial."[70]

3. New Initiatives in Sacramental Theology

Every theology must acknowledge that the Eucharist rests on Jesus' command of institution, which describes the Eucharist as a memorial of the Last Supper. Thus the Eucharist must be understood as a memorial of the Last Supper. But the Last Supper is Jesus' anticipation of his ultimate self-abandonment to the Father in his body surrendered and his blood shed on the cross. This, however, is not the end of Jesus of Nazareth. He is risen. His resurrection is part of his self-surrender in his departure to the Father. The Eucharist is given as the memorial of the Lord's death and resurrection. Hence the interpretation of the Eucharist must proceed from its character as memorial.

This idea must, therefore, be normative for all statements about the Eucharist. Attempts to make the sacrament and the sacramental action understandable can be developed within this framework. The Eucharist can be described in terms of linguistic philosophy as a performative action. As a memorial celebration, the Eucharist in the form of a meal can be seen as a figure of communicative action.[71] The meaning of memorial can certainly be more accurately explored by a philosophy of religion that accepts the traditions of faith.[72] On the other hand, the Eucharist and the sacraments in general can be presented as forms of encounter between God and human beings within the framework of Christ's memorial.[73] Herbert Vorgrimler retains the idea of effective symbolic event in his interpretation

---

[70] Odo Casel, "Mysteriengegenwart," *JLW* 8 (1929) 145–224, at 176.

[71] Cf. Alexandre Ganoczy, *Einführung in die katholische Sakramentenlehre* (Darmstadt, 1984), 106ff.; idem, "Neuzugänge zur Sakramentenlehre," in: *Ausdrucksgestaltungen des Glaubens. Zur Frage der Lebensbedeutung der Sakramente,* edited by the Akademie der Diözese Rottenburg/Stuttgart (Ostfildern, 1986) 51–63.

[72] Cf. Richard Schaeffler, "Darum sind wir eingedenk," above.

[73] Lothar Lies, *Sakramententheologie. Eine personale Sicht* (Graz, 1990); idem, "Kultmysterium heute: Modell sakramentaler Begegnung," *ALW* 28 (1986) 2–21.

of the sacraments, and therefore of the Eucharist also. In his understanding, symbols are grasped and interpreted in light of faith.[74]

The interpretation of the Eucharist must proceed from the command of institution and, in harmony with the liturgy and with the theology of the Fathers and Thomas Aquinas, the Eucharist must be primarily and fundamentally understood as the memorial celebration of the death and resurrection of the Lord.

4. Conclusion

The resurrection of Jesus Christ has ruptured the inevitabilities of history, including death. The Risen One is henceforth continually present to history. In our grateful remembrance, he and his work can become present.

In the celebration of the Eucharist, the participants in the thanksgiving made possible by the Spirit remind God the Father of what he has done for human beings in the Son. Christ, who is with the faithful, brings this memory before the Father. The Father reminds the assembled faithful of what he has done through the Son and makes his saving action effective for the faithful.

[74] Herbert Vorgrimler, *Sakramententheologie*. Leitfaden Theologie 17 (Düsseldorf, 1986). Translated by Linda M. Maloney under the title *Sacramental Theology* (Collegeville: The Liturgical Press, 1991).

Philipp Harnoncourt

4. "Te Deum Laudamus . . . ."

Divine Praise: A Fundamental Form of Christian Existence

Recent experiences with political developments and events in the East: the fall of the Berlin Wall, the disappearance of the Iron Curtain, the collapse of an evil ideology and dictatorship that despised human beings—these things offer an opportune background for understanding the subject of this essay. We all know that, why, and how we give thanks and praise when, unexpectedly and undeservedly, we receive the saving gift that brings us joy: the gift of life in freedom and peace.

This knowledge also determines the organization of my reflections: (1) What is praise? (2) Why do we praise God? and (3) How should we praise God? In a final part (4) I will say something about music and song as special forms of praise in the Church's worship.

I. What Is Praise?

What are we really talking about? Praise and exultation are only possible as reactions to something we have experienced. But not everything we experience is an occasion for us to give praise. Josef Pieper has defined the context of what we are talking about in this way: We must experience something as an "assent to life," to *our own* life, in fact really and always to *my own* life, before we find it necessary to give praise, to offer thanks, to celebrate. This reaction contains a fundamental assent: it is good that this exists, it is glorious that I have been able to experience it!

Loving Praise and Memorial Thanksgiving. But praise implies not only an experienced fact, a "something," but—and this is crucial—a "you" who has brought about this life-affirming experience that deserves celebration. Then our reaction is: It is good, it is glorious that "you" exist. Then we can sense something that Klemens Richter has mentioned: *praising* has something to do with *loving*: It is good that you exist, that I have met you, that I have been able to get to know you, that I can thank you for this or that. Immediately we perceive a second connection: *thanking* and *thinking*, giving thanks and remembering also belong together. Praise is thanksgiving, and giving thanks presupposes remembering. This memory also makes it possible for past experience, including the experience of other people, continually and ever anew to become our own experience.

Where the experience of salvation, as a personal experience of well-being, of happiness, and of life is totally lacking, there is no praise. Or, to say it the other way around: where there is no praise it appears that there is also no experience that makes people happy. How is it possible that, at one and the same time, some people are experiencing salvation and others are not? Probably some people understand particular events and experiences as the undeserved gifts of a good giver, while others see them only as a matter of course or as happy accidents. But it is also possible for our ability to experience to be crippled for various reasons.

Praise and Self-Congratulation. To make clear what it means to give praise, I would like to pose a second question: what is self-congratulation? There are people who think: what a lucky thing that I exist! These people believe they are the best thing that ever happened to those around them. But self-congratulation or self-praise is a demonic thing. People who have not only praised themselves and their own work, but have also ordered others to praise them, have usually brought horrible misery to humankind.

Self-praise can be expression of the fact that one does not wish to thank anyone else for oneself or to feel dependent on anyone; that one does not wish to receive anything from anyone, because one wishes to assert one's own rights and claims. Self-congratulation is a sign of blindness, and it also blinds.

Praise and Adoration. Praise becomes adoration when the "you" who is praised is God, and when this God is praised and glorified for God's own sake—because God is and remains holy, eternal, good, faithful, and devoted to us, and because we experience God in this way.

It is unfortunate that we theologians have increasingly shifted our relations with God from the realm of live experience to that of the mind. Confessions of faith that were embedded in adoring praise have become doctrines of faith that must be accepted by acts of will and obedience. But this kind of reflection and assent does not, as a rule, lead to praise. The latter emerges from our being affected by our own experience or by encounter with credible testimony of such experience. For Christians, the place for such witness is the celebration of the liturgy.

Praise in Community Celebration. Praise and thanksgiving are concretely realized and perceptible in celebration. And we speak of "celebration" when praise and thanksgiving are carried out ritually and in community. This celebration is (or is not!) an expression of experience and makes possible a renewed experience through grateful memory and loving praise. Therefore it again evokes praise and thanksgiving, which in turn can create further experience of God's grace and fidelity.

In the Church's celebrations, the Father is acknowledged as the one who is to be praised through Christ in the Spirit; the Son is also worthy of praise, as Lord, in the Spirit; and the Spirit is praiseworthy as well. To the Three-in-One we owe adoration, praise, and thanksgiving.

Adoration, praise, and thanksgiving are always *answering* (responsive, reactive) actions. This is true in the personal and individual sphere as well as in the liturgical assembly. And it is true of spontaneous reactions in the history of salvation as well as for their ritualized form in the liturgy. Praise is, therefore, by its very essence bound up in the entirety of a dynamic dialogue that occurs analogously in salvation history and in the liturgy.

Praise in the Dialogue of Salvation.

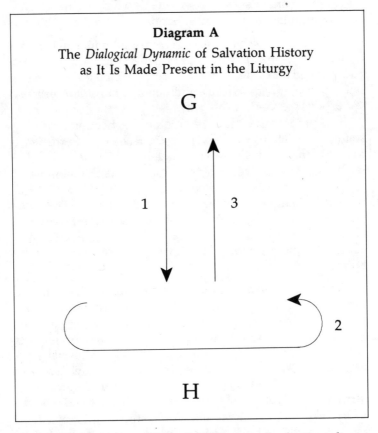

Diagram A

The *Dialogical Dynamic* of Salvation History
as It Is Made Present in the Liturgy

G

1   3

2

H

The primary initiative in the dialogue of salvation always proceeds from God: God (G) turns toward human beings (H). All praise and prayer is therefore a response. However, I have deliberately not represented this dialogue in only two directions, upward and downward, because this dialogue is not a game of ping-pong; it is an effective process that alters the human situation. God's turning toward humankind releases an effect on the human side: it touches the human person, and that effect, that situation of being-touched, is an experience that binds together those affected by it. When God turns toward human beings like a father or mother, human beings also experience themselves as sisters and brothers beloved of God.

It is this common experience of being touched by God that causes them to respond directly in praise and thanksgiving. This sequence—God turns to us (1), we are affected and know that we are affected (2), we respond out of our sense of God's touching us (3)—is characteristic of God's self-revelation as attested in salvation history among Jews, Christians, and Muslims. But there are religions whose ideas of the God-human dialogue reveal a different dynamic.

We also find the succession that is customary for us in the dialogue of salvation and the dynamic it expresses in our liturgy. In particular, the three constitutive forms of text—*reading, song, and prayer*—follow precisely this dynamic sequence: in the reading we experience God's turning toward us (1), in song we express our feeling of being touched by God's action (2), and our response becomes one of praise, thanksgiving, and adoration when it rises up in an expression of our consciousness of salvation (3). Singing is thus especially the form by which we express our common sense of being touched by God's actions (we sing before God), but also, in the second instance, an expression of direct response to God. *Te Deum laudamus* is therefore both praise and prayer.

Praise as an Act of Faith. Praise and prayer distinguish the form of faith that is most appropriate toward a God who is good, holy, and living. Accordingly, "orthodoxia" means first and literally *the right way of praising;* only later did the word acquire the meaning of right belief and right teaching. A further reflection of this fact is that the first three Church councils formulated their dogmas as "confessional formulas" or "creeds"—in a singable form!—while the dogmas of later councils were articulated as "doctrinal formulae" that were no longer intended to be sung.

Orthodox faith is expressed in adoration and confession. The "truth" of faith is not in the first instance founded on the correctness of a verbal statement about God, since in any case our human capacity for understanding and speech will always be inadequate to grasp or fully express God's infinity. The "truth" of faith consists primarily in the truthfulness of our response to the living God and our awareness of the reverence due to God. Hence we may say that when God is not (or is no longer) praised and adored, God is not the God of the covenant for and with us, and we cannot speak of true faith. For that reason it is silly to try to determine via questionnaire "what Germans (or Americans) believe," that is, what role religious faith still plays in our society, as, for example, a poll run by the Allensbacher Institute did some years ago. Answers to questions like: "Do you believe in a life after death?" are closely dependent on the situation of those questioned at the time (freedom from care, difficulties, despair, sorrow, etc.). Probably the uttering of a *Kyrie*, an *Alleluia*, or a *Sanctus* is a more essential confession of faith than some verbal assent to propositions in the catechism.

II. Why and for What Purpose Do We Praise God?

Here we will inquire about the reason for and the purpose of giving praise. "Why?" and "for what purpose?" are not the same question, and therefore do not seek the same answer.

"Why" asks about the cause(s) and reason(s), and therefore poses a causal question; "for what purpose" asks about direction and goal, the intention and meaning, including also effects and consequences as well: therefore it asks a question about finality.

1. The reasons for praise and celebration

Why do we praise God? Why *must* we praise God? The answer will probably be easier to find if, following a train of thought we established in the first part of this essay, we ask: why is there celebration? Why *must* we celebrate?

In Austrian dialect we have a powerful expression: "Des muaß g'feiert werd'n!" ("That *has* to be celebrated!") In particular situations people are spontaneously and unanimously sure that something has to be celebrated right away. When does that certainty arise? We are interested primarily in the question about the "what" it is that needs celebrating, and that of the feeling of obligation: this "must-celebrate."

The Experience of Salvation. We can refer to the reason already given by Josef Pieper: events and persons are worthy of celebration when they are experienced as "assent to life," and this frequently happens in situations in which our life appears to be under extreme stress. It is easy to understand that a soccer team and its fans will celebrate a victory just won, and that when we have passed an examination or have been restored to health after a severe illness, we will want to celebrate. In the Gospel of Luke, the recovery of the lost sheep, the lost coin, and the lost son (chapter 15) are introduced as events that must, as a matter of course, be celebrated: "Rejoice with me!"

But if life-threatening or life-destroying events like death, natural catastrophes, or war are seen as occasions for celebration, it is not the events themselves that are celebrated or worth celebrating, but the assent to life that is so important to us when life is threatened or destroyed. On the occasion of sickness and death it is life that is celebrated; in war, it is peace, and in the face of every evil ("Unheil"), it is the good ("Heil") that is celebrated. Only in this way can we celebrate at all. It may be that, if a basis in faith is lacking, even the solidarity of the celebrating community itself may be an adequate experience of good, of salvation.

Salvation Through the Mystery of Christ. It is a fact that in the liturgy Christians, as Church, always celebrate the ultimate assent to life that was accomplished in the incarnation, death, and resurrection of Christ.

Since this event worthy of celebration is, from an historical point of view, distant from our immediate experience, we must refer in this case to a unique characteristic of *memorial celebrations*: they have the power to mediate anew the experience that is the cause of the celebration, so that in a memorial celebration there can be a new experience of what it is that makes this event worth celebrating. This is especially important in the feasts that make up the cycle of the Church's year. This "experiencing anew" is rooted not only in our ability to remember, or in the hearing of what happened before, the good effects of which extend to the present time—as may be the case with secular memorials—but is based on the faith conviction that Christ, with his life and his work, has by his resurrection been elevated to God's eternity and therefore is always and at every moment present, i.e., "contemporary. ' We celebrate and experience not something that is past, but something present, and in celebrating we are contemporary with our salvation with Christ and in the Holy Spirit.

Thus we celebrate Christmas and Easter not only because Jesus was born at some time in the past and rose at some time or other, but because his incarnation and resurrection accompany us and because, in the celebration, we can experience his incarnation and resurrection anew. In the celebration we should and can experience our salvation in Christ as happening here and now for us (and for me) and that we (and I) are incorporated into this event.

The Creation Praises Its Creator. Our praise has a broader, existential basis that precedes every Christian experience of salvation. All creatures have their being and, if they are living things, their life is not from themselves and therefore is not for themselves. No creature has control of existence and life, and yet it is and lives.

Whence come our existence and our life? There can be only two answers to this question: either existence and life are the results of meaningless accident, or they are willed and produced by a personal Other, a Creator.

If we suppose that there is a personal Other, we can say: we are, we exist, we live, because another, a Creator, wants us to be. Creatures owe their existence to a creator and, as creatures, they are always dependent. What is our attitude toward that? Is this dependency degrading, or is it a source of comfort, peace, and joy? If one can rely completely on another, is that degrading, or is it blissful?

In general, every human being finds the experience of being able to rely on someone else as something wonderful. People who can trust in no one and nothing, who must rely only on themselves, will always live in fear: fear that something will be done to them, or that they will lose something, even their very selves.

It is worth noting that this phrase "to rely on" describes the only behavior in which we set aside our "ego," and still retain a positive attitude. Words like "self-denial," "self-renunciation," "self-conquest," "self-mortification" are negatively weighted and are burdened with the idea of having to inflict something on oneself. Even the one who "relies on . . ." must do something to the self, for in order for the "on . . ." to be possible at all, one first has to "rely," that is, let go of oneself and place oneself in another's hands. To be able to relax while another carries us, holds us in existence and keeps us alive because that one loves us is immensely liberating. It relieves us from all fear over our existence and gives us peace and security in absolute trust.

Children who feel themselves secure in the care of their parents have this attitude. It is only in this attitude that children can flourish. That is why Jesus put a child in the midst of his disciples and commanded them to become like such a one. "Unless you change and become like children, you will never enter the kingdom of heaven" (Matt 18:3). Faith in God, in an existential sense, means this kind of letting oneself go, of trusting in God, knowing oneself safe in God; it means letting go of the idea that we have to take care of everything ourselves. It therefore means giving joyful assent to one's own creatureliness, relying on one's creator and praising, glorifying and thanking God the creator.

Praise of the creator is a grateful assent to creatureliness, assent to the fact that I owe myself to another, that I am dependent on another, but at the same time am supported by the knowledge that I am not simply cast out into nothingness, but am made to live and to share in the life of the creator. My created self includes not only my past, but also my present and future, a fantastic future. It is a gift that brings great joy.

The Covenant People Praises the Covenant God. The experiences of God's mighty deeds in history are such as to occasion praise of God. First and primary among these mighty works of God in the history of the covenant people was the creation itself. God spoke the effective "let there be . . .," and God continues to say "let there be. . . ." That I am and live today is a sign that God says "let there be . . ." even today. In the context of our existence as created beings it is very important that we take seriously this connection and unity of past, present, and future, which we have already mentioned with regard to the mystery of Christ, for all God's mighty works. Among them are creation, promise, covenant, salvation . . . and in every case with a view to completion. God says yes to us in love, that is, in my own personal experience as well, and God remains faithful to himself and his work.

An essential part of the praise of God in the midst of the covenant people is the continually repeated acclamation: "Bless God, whose mercy endures forever!" It is to be found countless times in the Book of Psalms. "Mercy" is God's saving care, and "endures forever" praises the irrevocability of God's care for us. Mercy marks the vertical bond between God and human beings, fidelity the horizontal bond through time. God's mercy and fidelity can be experienced and must be praised, because they cause us to live, and they give us meaning, salvation, and a future.

God's Fidelity and Human Infidelity. God's fidelity desires to be answered by the fidelity of the covenant partner. This fidelity of the creature, the human being, reveals itself to be very fragile. Thus from God's point of view the history of salvation is also repeatedly experienced as human anti-salvational history, the history of disaster. Human beings think they will lose their freedom if they assent to their dependence on God. They want to be like God, create their own happiness and praise themselves. But what they create for themselves is death, the ruin of love, the destruction of fidelity, the devastation of the covenant, and the wreck of their future.

The creature can only be creature, or not be at all. The creature that desires to take (that is, possess) its own life, takes its own life indeed (that is, kills itself). But even in the face of suicidal human infidelity, God's fidelity reveals itself as irrevocable. God remains true to his "yes, let there be. . . ." The creator is revealed as savior.

The basis and the reason for praising God is not *knowledge* of God's mercy and fidelity, but the actual *experience* of being touched by them. This experience of God can, of course, be combined with anxiety. We should also look for our salvation "in fear and trembling." It is not self-evident that the repeated infidelity of the covenant partner will not affect God's fidelity. The holy God is also a righteous judge.

The Obligation to Praise. Among the reasons "why" we praise God, we should also mention our obligation to do so. Our old catechism, which I had to teach when I was a young assistant pastor and on which I was obliged to test the students, contained the question: "Why must we pray?" and the answer: "We must pray, first because God has commanded us to, and second because without prayer we cannot be happy." These answers were deficient, and the second was even false to the extent that it responds not to a "why," but to a "for what purpose" kind of question. The first answer, which of course is true also of praise, thanksgiving, and adoration, points up a dilemma: can praise, thanksgiving, and adoration take place if they are seen as the fulfilling of something we are commanded to do, and are carried out according to orders?

The "must" of the commandment—without questioning the commandment itself—has to be augmented or replaced by the "must" that arises from the experience of something worthy of celebration, of which we spoke earlier in this section. ("That *has* to be celebrated!") Praise, thanksgiving, and adoration, like every celebration, are strangers to any kind of requirement. And if we are carrying out orders against our will, we will not succeed in giving genuine praise. But in view of the holiness, the mercy, and the irrevocable fidelity of God, it would be irresponsible of us to surrender our praises to the casual spontaneity of consciously experienced events. Fidelity—that is, fidelity that is experienced and is owed in turn—is also aware of binding obligation and is therefore entrusted to our will.

I recall, at this point, a saying that my grandmother gave me when I entered the seminary:

> I slept, and I dreamed
>   that life is happiness.
> I woke, and I saw
>   that life is duty.
> I acted, and behold:
>   duty is happiness.

Those who owe it to God and the world to praise God remain obligated before God, the world, and themselves.

After this description of the reasons for our praise, we must briefly address the question of the meaning and goal of such praise.

2. The Meaning and Effects of Praise and Celebration

For what purpose should we praise God? God, after all, does not depend on our praise; God gains nothing by our praise and loses nothing if we refuse to give it.

Glorifying God Benefits Human Beings and the World. We arrive here at an apparent paradox: although, and even because human beings set themselves aside when they glorify God, making God the center of their attention and action toward God, responding to God's mercy, the one who benefits from the praise of God is the human being. In carrying out the dialogue of salvation, humans take the place that belongs to them as those created by God, saved by God, and sheltered in the love of God. ". . . those who hate their life in this world will keep it for eternal life" (John 12:25). "No one has greater love [that is, more intensive, more perfect life] than this, to lay down one's life for one's friends" (John 15:13). Those who give up their "I" to praise God find themselves again, blessed. Those who "lose themselves in God" return to themselves in God. Thus the praise of God brings the fullness of salvation and blessing into the world, in a way that humanity cannot accomplish by the most strenuous effort.

In praising God, the human being remains safe, whole ("heil") and saved ("im Heil"). In praising the creator, the creature remains aware of its creatureliness, that it is standing over against its Lord, owing that Lord not only praise, but obedience as well, responsible before the Lord for fellow human beings and for the environment. Salvation must remain salvation, life must remain life, and peace, reconciliation, freedom, God's great saving gifts, must remain what they are.

We are not to praise God out of fear that God might withdraw the gift of mercy, but when we cease to praise God we are guilty because we lose our awareness of our place as created and redeemed people sheltered in God's mercy.

Refusal to Glorify God Destroys Humanity and the World. In my interpretation of history, the French Revolution and, later, the October Revolution in Russia are signs that people no longer wanted to accept or thought that they should accept God's saving gifts in gratitude, but instead believed that human beings could and would create for themselves the saving gifts that the Gospel knows only as the gifts of God: freedom, equality, brotherhood and sisterhood. There was the further assertion that the Church had by no means distributed these saving gifts to the people. Were these revolutions only a protest against God, to whom people no longer wished to be grateful, or were they also signs that the Church was no longer a witness and guarantor of these gifts of salvation and liberation for everyone? Did the churches not, in fact, spiritualize the saving gifts of God, deferring salvation to the end of time and thus resigning themselves to the continuing existence of inequality, unloving relationships, injustice, and violence here and now?

In any case, praising God and not praising God have not only salvation-historical, but also historical consequences. I think we can sense that with particular immediacy at the present time.

III. How Should We Praise God?

With regard to this "how," I would like to say at the outset that the way in which we live nowadays makes a joyful experience of salvation more difficult than in the past. We must therefore take care, when considering the question "how should we praise?" that the possibilities for experiencing salvation remain open.

Obstacles to a Deep Experience of Salvation

Why is it that our way of life makes opportunities for a deep experience of salvation so difficult to find, or even blocks them out altogether? *Haste* and *superficiality* are obstacles to deep experience. Haste and superficiality—we may think, for example, of the overcoming of great distances by the airplane, railroad, and automobile—make it impossible for us to experience what land and nature are. We see things only fleetingly; one impression banishes the next, and is immediately replaced by still another. When we go on foot and linger to observe, we can occupy ourselves with many details, take pleasure in them and allow them to sink in. Of course, a plane trip also opens up new experiences because it can allow us to feel something of the immensity of the earth and—if we fly at night—even the measureless depths of the universe. But the modern motto, "faster, faster, faster" is a hindrance to deep experience. The *massive scale* of many events, and the flood of information, are further obstacles to enduring experience.

The encounter with death is one of the most important of the experiences that introduce for us the questions of God and God's goodness, to the extent that we really confront them. In a family circle death occurs relatively seldom, so that it can be experienced deeply and enduringly. But if we are constantly confronted by masses of dead or seriously wounded people in news broadcasts, television images, or even in traffic accidents we ourselves witness, a deep engagement with them is impossible. We are shocked for a moment, and then the next news segment follows. In traffic one can experience it very clearly, if one should drive past dead or injured people lying in the street (I myself have had this experience several times): the curious want to stop and look; the police wave at us: go on, go on; nearly everyone drives slowly for the next few kilometers because they have been shocked by the sight of someone dead. But soon we speed up again, and after no more than twenty kilometers we are driving as if we had seen nothing. We cannot do otherwise. I imagine that even nurses and emergency medical technicians who deal with dead and dying people every day cannot experience death and aid the dying with the same personal feeling that is possible within the family.

Thus there are circumstances in our life today that restrict our ability to experience, and that especially block out the deep personal feelings that are indispensable for praise. We must therefore take great care to see that deep experiences of salvation remain available.

Recollection, Amazement, and Silence. We are in debt to Romano Guardini for the important statements he made in many of his writings. Especially in his book *Besinnung vor der Feier der heiligen Messe*, first published at Mainz in 1939, Guardini points to the attitudes of *stillness, silence, and recollection* that he regarded as indispensable preconditions for ''participation'' in the liturgy. They are also preconditions for genuine praise.

Unlike all the loud and jangling sensations that remain superficial, no matter how strong they are, the depths of experience open to us only in *stillness* and *patient waiting*. First we must withdraw from all haste and hurry and achieve some *quiet repose*; then we must *collect* our senses, which are open in every direction, and our distracted thoughts—that is, we must bring them together and concentrate them on one thing; and finally, we must remain present to ourselves and, once collected, move outside ourselves in order to grasp that one thing and remain attentive to it.

Only those who have learned to remain with one object, in stillness and recollection—be it a thing, a word, an experience, a person—and to surrender themselves to that one, can begin to *be amazed*, that is, to allow themselves to be totally gripped by this one thing or this one person. After some practice, stillness and recollection will show us very quickly what will repay our attention, because it is full for us and can fill us, and which things are empty and vapid and therefore leave us empty as well. What matters to me, what does not matter to me? Only that which amazes me can ultimately awaken my praise.

The mighty deeds of God evoke amazement, as do the words and miracles of Jesus, as told to us in the Old and New Testaments. ". . . the crowd was *amazed* when they saw the mute speaking, the maimed whole, the lame walking, and the blind seeing. And they praised the God of Israel" (Matt 15:31).

The first effect of amazement is *falling silent*. Anyone who is amazed will first cease speaking. We say: "she was struck dumb!" Genuine praise breaks forth out of silence, never out of noise. The old saying, "tibi silentium laus" ("to you, O God, silence is praise") can be understood in a number of ways:

1) The whole lifeless creation praises God in ways we cannot hear: "Light and stone praise you gloriously in silence" (G. Thurmair).

2) Praise can only arise from silent amazement, but it must ascend to the level of audible jubilation so that the praise may be made public.

3) Even the loudest jubilation ultimately ends in satisfied silence.

I cannot accept the third interpretation, for, according to the testimony of the Book of Revelation, continual, audible and visible rejoicing is part of the perfection and completion of all things.

Repeated Memorial Celebrations. Concern for genuine praise implies also concern for a proper *memoria.* Enduring memory is perfected primarily in the cyclically returning memorial celebrations of God's mighty deeds:

> In the weekly "eucharistia" (i.e., literally, praise) on Sunday;
> In the daily Liturgy of the Hours, in which morning and evening prayer are the principal celebrations;
> In the annual memorial celebrations of the Lord, the mother of God, and the saints.

What is this regular repetition intended to do? The liturgical reforms of Vatican II have brought repetition somewhat into disrepute because the reformers recommended that "unnecessary duplications" be done away with. What was meant by this was, in the first instance, those doublings imposed on the celebrant (in the readings and chants); these were to be eliminated, but by no means was it intended that all repetitions should be removed. The cyclically recurring celebrations just mentioned would be unimaginable were it not that repetition is the principle of memorial celebration.

It is only repetition that makes possible and effects a deepening of experience within the fleeting transitoriness of time. This deepening is effected according to the principle of the screw or spiral. If the threads are in alignment, the screw, although it appears the same, is actually driven deeper with every turn.

In the recurrence of familiar celebrations, we experience things we have already experienced, but always in a new way, for two reasons:

> 1) The same message finds us each time in a new situation in the history of our own lives and of our world. (In Germany, that was easy to see as Easter 1988 was followed by Easter 1989 and Easter 1990!) The message is illuminated and interpreted anew in each new situation. The reverse is also true:

2) The message itself is so many-layered and so freighted with meaning that it opens itself to us only through repeated celebrations, gradually, and in deeper and deeper ways.

None of us, even though we may have celebrated Easter fifty times, feels boredom as the next Easter approaches because we have known "everything" about it for a long time now; instead, we look forward to it in joy because in it we will be given a new experience and a deeper understanding. This does not depend on new and surprising sensations and rituals in the celebration, which often tend rather to distract us, but on a new encounter with the familiar. If our experience of salvation is deeper, so also our praise will be more solid, lasting, and genuine.

We should not ignore the danger that regular repetition may also lead to a kind of bloating and depreciation of value. The danger will be greater the more trivial and superficial the repeated elements of the celebration are in themselves or in their execution, and the shorter the cycles of repetition. It is easier for daily morning prayer to grow flat than for the annual Easter feast to do so. On the other hand, the experience of the Jesus prayer in the Eastern Church shows that the cyclic repetition of the simplest forms in the shortest rhythm (breathing and heartbeat) can lead to the most intensive concentration and deepening.

. . . *with unlimited exuberance.* Intensive praise goes hand in hand with self-forgetfulness. This self-forgetfulness expresses itself in unlimitedness, exuberance, the abandonment of purpose and utility, wastefulness, extravagance. . . . The thrifty, careful rationalist and the calculating egoist shake their heads: "why this extravagance?" Jesus' disciples asked the same question when the woman poured a jar of expensive ointment over Jesus' head (Matt 26:8). Jesus said: "You will not always have me," and "the wedding guests cannot fast while the bridegroom is with them" (cf. Mark 2:19).

Limitless exuberance in praise and celebration is the appropriate response to God's infinity, surpassing all understanding, and to the overflowing generosity of God's saving gifts both in time and in eternity.

. . . with music and song. The question of "how to" praise is related in a special way to the language of music. Singing and making music are the forms of expression that are fitting for praise because singing is human beings' adequate expression of deep feeling, of sensitivity and of those things that are impossible to say. It is, in particular, the expressions of salvation and of joy that are not susceptible of utterance in verbal-linguistic forms, unless that language is "condensed" into art. The historical aspect of these experiences can be described and put into words, but the feeling of being touched by salvation cannot. Ludwig Wittgenstein coined the saying: "We must be silent about the things we cannot say." As Christians, we can alter that saying in a fundamental way: If there are things we cannot say, we can sing or make music about them; in fact we *have* to sing when we must not or even cannot be silent.

By *music* we mean the musical expression that is not combined with words, while by *song* we mean a mysterious combination of verbal-linguistic expression and non-verbal vocalization. For Jews and Christians, song is particularly important just because of this combination of speech and melody. In speech, that is, in the text of the song, it is clear what has happened, and that God has turned toward human beings in history, in events that can and must be documented, can and must be described. I can read about them, I can talk about them, but I can and must sing about them as well.

The experiences of salvation have content and therefore can be verbally expressed, but as experiences of *salvation* they have touched human beings in the center of their persons, rescued them from their existential anxiety, and opened for them a vista of hope and of the future. They have caused them to experience God's love and awakened their love for God. This cannot be expressed in words. This existential dimension of faith calls for an expression arising from the center of the person and giving credible expression to deep feeling. "Cantare amantis est," said Augustine (d. 430): song is the language of love; anyone who loves must sing. Thus Christian faith needs song as an adequate sign of grateful acceptance of the gift of salvation, in praise of the Savior and in gratitude for the assurance of already possessing a share, with the community of all believers, in the eternal future.

IV. Singing and Making Music in the Church's Liturgy

Divine praise appears nowhere more clearly than in liturgical song and music.

1. Music is the Language of Emotions and the Speech of the Gods

The importance of song and music is associated with the two oldest theories about the origins of music, both of which have survived to the present and are found in nearly all cultures. *Music is the language of the emotions, or as we also say: the language of the heart.* That is why human beings spontaneously produce music. Before all verbal speech, our voice provides us with a means of expression that is instinctively used and understood, for every viable newborn can and must express itself with its voice, giving utterance to health, joy in existence, joy in being loved and accepted, but also to pain, fear, and suffering. Out of this behavior, the use of the voice, and with the differentiated development of "vocal life-capacities," the musical world develops together with the life of the spirit, the inner world of feelings. Praise needs music if it is to be praise.

The second theory of origins says that *music is the language of the universe, or also the language of the gods.* Human beings find music already existing outside them. They hear the song of birds, the rushing of the wind, the splashing of water. . . . They think that the whole universe is a sounding thing, that the beauty and harmony of music echo the beauty of the universe and are derived from it. Human beings have either received music as a gift from the gods, or they have stolen it from them.

To the extent that human beings believe in a creator god, music is seen as an expression of the divine beauty and harmony, and for Christians a chord reflects the Three-in-One, the Trinity. According to this theory of its origin, music is also the *language of the angels* who glorify and adore God. Our songs and our music are thus the form of praise that responds to God's glory, and at the same time a participation in the angels' praise (see all the Prefaces in the missal!). To the extent that other creatures cannot sing, our singing and making music is also praise in the name of the entire creation: "With our tongues all creatures laud you and proclaim the praise of your glory!'' (Fourth Eucharistic Prayer in the German missal). Through our music, the voiceless praise of the universe becomes audible to all that have ears to hear.

In our sung praise to God our spontaneous jubilation becomes conscious and deliberate praise; our unconscious participation in the creation's praise of its creator becomes a conscious and deliberate fulfilling of our duty, and our unconscious sharing in God's harmony becomes a conscious and deliberate attuning of ourselves to God's triune life.

2. *Singing and Making Music Is a Highly Effective Form of Communication.*

The Communication Process. While most of the newer models of communication are di-polar, describing only the event that takes place between the communicators (sender and receiver), the model I prefer is Karl Bühler's (from his 1936 book, *Sprachtheorie*). It is tri-polar and pays attention also to the content of the communication.

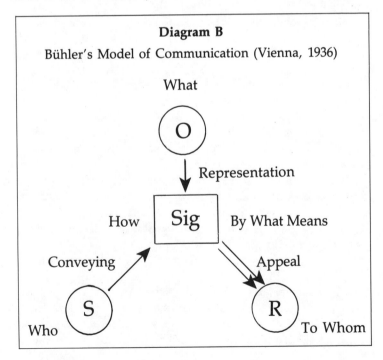

Diagram B

Bühler's Model of Communication (Vienna, 1936)

One person (the *sender* = S) conveys something (a fact or an *object* = O) to another person (the *receiver* = R), and does so by means of a *signal* (Sig). This whole process can be briefly illustrated in the form of a question: *who* conveys *what* to *whom* and *how*? The precondition for any communication is that the partners in the communication are capable of expression and perception.

The *signal,* as an indispensable means of communication, has a particular relationship to each of the three poles:

It is *conveyance,* expression, utterance, self-communication for the sender;

It is *representation* for the object,

It is *appeal,* impression, information for the recipient.

The received, informative signal that the recipient takes in as an impression brings with it two clusters of information which she or he, by concentrating attention on the signal, filters out either consciously or unconsciously. There is information about something, and there is personal information about the sender, for the latter not only conveys something different from her- or himself, but always communicates something of the self as well. The sender's self-communication should be truthful, the representation of the object correct and appropriate, and the appeal to the recipient comprehensible and informative.

Most processes of communication between human beings employ verbal speech as their signaling system. But what is represented by this model is also true of song and music. Those who sing and make music express themselves together with something different from themselves, and both messages are communicated to the hearers. In singing, the self-communication is produced by the voice (and movement) and thus conveys "mood" and emotion at the same time; the factual information is conveyed by the text. In music without text, the same thing occurs in principle, but the factual information is more difficult to decipher. It is easy to tell from the manner of singing whether that about which the singer sings applies to him- or herself. One can tell whether, as indicated, *something* is being sung, that is, "Song Number . . .," or whether someone wants to sing and must sing because he or she is in the mood.

But the most enthusiastic and spirited singing can be a failure if the musical form is not apprópriate to the content, the thing which, or about which, the singer is singing.

Praise to God, honor and thanks for God's mighty deeds and the adoration of the Holy place demands on the musical form of the songs that are as inflexible as those imposed by the uniqueness of those singing and hearing. Even the kinds of singing and making music at divine worship that are said to be adapted to children or youth must not ignore the issue of what is appropriate to the encounter with God in each particular instance. It may be an unmistakable expression of the fact that a relationship to God is simply lacking, or that essential qualities are absent. If, for example, the musical form is superficial, the best text cannot strike a deep chord because those singing and those hearing are kept at a surface level by the music and their movement to a deeper level is thereby blocked off.

The effectiveness of musical communication. Music informs us (in a quite literal sense) unconsciously and with intense effect. Its voice expresses a mood, awakens that mood in the hearers, and creates accord. But how does that happen?

The way in which musical communication is effected is best illustrated by the familiar interplay of *sonance* and *resonance*. Every tone is evoked and reproduced by a particular set of vibrations; if it encounters an object with an equal capacity for vibration, the latter immediately begins to vibrate in sympathy, and the tone is taken up and amplified. Sonance finds resonance if the frequency is right. That is just what we mean when good friends express their accord by saying: "We are on the same wavelength."

Every kind of music has its own sonance and evokes the corresponding resonance. (Something similar may be said of every art form.) In this, what people are accustomed to hearing and other socio-cultural circumstances play a major role. The capacity of human beings for sonance and resonance is not, in the first place, a question of artistic gift, but of the cultivation of sensibility and the development of the spirit.

As human understanding develops hand in hand with the capacity for verbal speech, so also our emotional facilities and capacity develop along with our musical and overall artistic activity. A school system in which musical and artistic training are given too little attention, or none at all, produces people whose emotional capacities remain underdeveloped.

Therefore, in order for music to function, we must take care that our capacity for resonance is broad; then we can vibrate with many tones. A harp is a very resonant instrument because there is a string for every tonal length. Anyone who sings with a harp notices that it vibrates without interruption because its corresponding vibrational capacities are at liberty. A great and varied capacity for vibration is born in human beings, but we must also cultivate that capacity for resonance.

Musical communication among human beings is, as a rule, strong and inescapable; it is beyond any deliberate direction. With the aid of music and song, people's feelings and movements can be harmonized and synchronized. Examples of this are marches, work songs, dance music, battle tunes, music for mourning, music for meditation, lullabies, and so on. The elementary factors at work are tension and release, as well as change and monotony.

Because, as we saw in the first section, community praise is characteristic of every celebration, music is an indispensable element of any festival: on the one hand because it is the mode of expression for every kind of praise, and on the other hand because it brings all the participants together to praise, awakens or intensifies their praise, and allows them to join in, until everyone is in accord. We will return to the idea that this must not be done in a manipulative way.

Changes in musical behavior caused by technical innovations. The invention of mechanical or electronic instruments has made great changes in musical behavior. Before the invention of apparatus that can reproduce music, one could only hear music when people played. Music was therefore always a special event. The technical production of music by tapes, discs, or synthesizers, and its constant availability, have made music an article of consumption that can be made use of at any time and that, as a result, has lost its character as event. For many people music has become an unavoidable racket and is no longer experienced, without further qualification, as something pleasant. Their justified desire for silence and repose in celebrations must be taken seriously.

It is a blessing that in the Church's worship the singing and music is almost always live, although in other celebrations, especially at dances, mechanically produced music has long been the rule.

The consumption of music as a drug ("Walkman!") is not something completely harmless, whether it is used for isolation, for flight, for the creation of an artificial world for oneself, or for the production of synthetic feelings of well-being that are no longer a reaction to the experience of salvation ("Heil"). Under such circumstances, praise is no longer possible.

3. The Place and Undergirding for Christians' Songs of Praise Is the Community Assembly.

Even if the choir sings during the liturgy, instead of the assembly, the community is not an "audience" listening to a presentation. It is the community that celebrates, delegating particular actions to the part of the community that is best able to carry them out. A community that ordinarily does its own singing knows that there are occasions and needs that call for a celebration carried out in special forms and drawing on all the available strengths of the group. Then the choir does not detract from the activity of the assembly, and when there is a harmonious relationship between the community and its choir individual members of the assembly will often exclaim: "Didnt *we* sing beautifully today?!"

Singing in the liturgy is the primary form of active participation by all believers. It characterizes the celebration as a whole and the participation of every individual as praise and thanksgiving, adoration and petition to God the Father through Christ in the Holy Spirit.

Singing in the liturgy is the expression of an existentially effective faith, a faith that is not primarily the assent to truths presented for belief, but faith put into effect as total surrender to God in gratitude for the experience of salvation. In singing the community shows *that* it believes, *whom* it believes, *what* it believes, and *how* it believes.

Singing makes the Church visible as a sign of salvation in this world and thus as an invitation to the world to join in the community of salvation.

Singing in the assembly serves the building up of the community and is thus a service of love that Christians give to each other. The enthusiastic and explosive exuberance of the singing, which seems to be a ritualized form of "speaking in tongues" (1 Cor 14), can detract from that service, so that we should always keep in mind Paul's admonition: "In church I would rather speak five words with my mind, in order to instruct others also, than ten thousand words in a tongue" (1 Cor 14:19).

The community's singing is always the work of the Spirit and therefore a sign of the presence and effective power of the Holy Spirit. The New Testament canticles in the Gospel of Luke are all connected with statements by and about the Spirit: Mary has conceived by the Holy Spirit, is greeted by Elizabeth as the mother of the Lord, and sings her song of praise, the *Magnificat*. Elizabeth is filled by the Holy Spirit and praises Mary; Zechariah is filled by the Holy Spirit and sings the *Benedictus*; and the communities at Ephesus and Colossae are told to "be filled with the Spirit as you sing psalms and hymns and spiritual songs among yourselves" (Eph 5:18-19; Col 3:16). The universally applicable saying: "enthusiasm (spirited emotion: German "Begeisterung," from "Geist," "spirit") makes you sing" attains its excess of theological meaning at this point.

For Israel and for Christians, music and singing in the celebrating community are also signs and pledges of heavenly glory. Song is the most spiritual of the arts, because it requires neither material nor instruments. Whenever heaven and heavenly glory are described, whether in words or in images, music is brought into the picture. The angels sing their "holy, holy, holy . . ." in adoration and praise, holding sheets of music or instruments in their hands. Singing, the community joins in the eternal hymn of praise.

God's covenant with human beings is a great betrothal aimed at God's marriage with humanity. In Jesus Christ, divinity and humanity have been irrevocably joined. Christ, the bridegroom, espouses the Church in the Eucharistic wedding banquet. So the Christian community's singing is the love song of the bride, the wedding song for the bridegroom, "for the marriage of the Lamb has come" (Rev 19:7).

4. *The Proof of the Truth of our Praise of God Is in the Witness of Christian Life.*

The Cultic Critique of the Prophets, and of Jesus. What has been said thus far appears to be an enthusiastic encouragement and endorsement of all songs of praise in Christian worship. But we should not be blind to the serious critique of worship practices, both by the Old Testament prophets and by Jesus in the New Testament.

We find the sharpest and most critical notes in the Book of Amos: "I hate, I despise your festivals, and I take no delight in your solemn assemblies! . . . Take away from me the noise of your songs; I will not listen to the melody of your harps!" (5:21, 23). "[You] sing idle songs to the sound of the harp, and like David improvise on instruments of music" (6:5). Similar words are found in the Book of Isaiah: ". . . bringing offerings is futile. . . . New moon and sabbath and calling of convocation—I cannot endure solemn assemblies with iniquity. Your new moons and your appointed festivals my soul hates; they have become a burden to me, I am weary of bearing them" (Is 1:13-14).

What is it that enrages God? The falseness and hypocrisy of an apparently intact cultic practice, while at the same time God is despised: "Your hands are full of blood! Wash yourselves; make yourselves clean; remove the evil of your doings from before my eyes! . . . learn to do good; seek justice, rescue the oppressed, defend the orphan, plead for the widow" (Is 1:16-17). Jesus' words are along the same line: "Not everyone who says to me, 'Lord, Lord,' will enter the kingdom of heaven, but only the one who does the will of my Father in heaven" (Matt 7:21).

These words should also alert Christians when we all too enthusiastically sing our "Kyrie" or adorn ourselves contentedly with songs of praise and liturgical busyness, but at the same time, without noticing it, forget to order our whole lives according to God's will.

At the final judgment, we will not be asked about our praise of God in the liturgy, and that will not be the criterion of decision; it will depend only on whether we have had pity on those in need (cf. Matt 25:31-46). Those who want to appeal to the fact that they are Jesus' disciples may hear: "I never knew you; go away from me, you evildoers!" (cf. Matt 7:22-23; Luke 13:26-27). The pre-eminent praise of God is the obedient doing of God's will. "I appeal to you therefore, brothers and sisters, by the mercies of God, to present your bodies as a living sacrifice, holy and acceptable to God, which is your spiritual worship" (Rom 12:1).

How can it happen that the necessary praise that is due to God is twisted into blasphemy? We must recognize the dangers in order to avoid them.

The dangers: complacency, triviality, silence. It is of the essence of festival joy, music, and art, that their excess and enthusiasm cause us to forget everything else. In the first instance we should see this as something positive, but in its tendency to *complacency* it conceals the danger that we will forget the ordering of praise to the one who is to be praised. Songs of praise and festival celebration become an aim in themselves, in the sense of a demand for "art for art's sake," when art exists for itself alone, free of any kind of finality or purpose outside itself. Then praise loses all meaning.

This kind of complacency necessarily leads to *triviality*, which is worse, because now truthfulness is lost as well. If nothing counts any longer but the external form, which was originally meant to be the expression of something internal, the internal itself can disappear or even be denied. Praise and thanksgiving become an alibi, a deception and self-deception: there is nothing and no one behind them any longer. Or, still worse, the form pretends that God is to be adored and glorified for his mighty deeds or for his own sake, but in fact what we are putting forward is ourselves, our abilities, our achievements, so that we ourselves may be praised and celebrated.

Almost all reform movements in the Church are reserved or negative toward art, because of the dangers of complacency and triviality, excess and vanity.

But the *silencing* of jubilee is also a danger. The apparent embrace of poverty and pure reason frequently reveals itself to be nothing but an insipid rationalism and forgetting of God. Nothing counts but what is rational and what is useful. Playing social responsibility off against the obligation to praise God can also lead rapidly to an isolation in pure self-sufficiency. "For you always have the poor with you, but you will not always have me" (Matt 26:11); with these words Jesus justifies irrational waste out of love for him. Those who have not learned to surrender themselves in grateful love to God, the Holy One, the Redeemer, will not be able to surrender themselves to the service of the poor.

Today's Critical Voices. Listening to Jesus' and the prophets' critique of worship, always contemporary as it is, should not make us deaf to critical voices that can be heard *today* and that show how current and important the question at issue remains, especially today.

Critics of the liturgical reforms of Vatican II complain that in the renewed celebrations there is too much talk and too little festive celebration and jubilee. Others, who should be taken with equal seriousness, such as Johann Baptist Metz, say: "I hear too much singing and too little screaming!"

Both voices should give us pause. When the praise of God falls silent, faith in God and love for God will vanish. When the cry of anguish is silenced, solidarity with and love for our fellow human beings are endangered, and ultimately so is hope in God's salvation.

We may, indeed we must wail, and we must praise, so that faith remains faith, and love is always love.

Additional Literature

Teresa Berger. *Theologie in Hymnen? Zum Verhältnis von Theologie und Doxologie am Beispiel der Collection of Hymns for the use of the "People Called Methodists."* Münsteraner Theologische Abhandlungen 6. Altenberge: Telos Verlag, 1989.

Daniel W. Hardy and David F. Ford. *Jubilate: Theology in Praise.* London: Darton, Longman and Todd, 1984.

Philipp Harnoncourt. "Die liturgische und apostolische Sendung der Musica Sacra," *Heiliger Dienst* 43 (1989) 49–71.

Geoffrey Wainwright. *Doxology: The Praise of God in Worship, Doctrine, and Life. A Systematic Theology.* New York: Oxford University Press, 1984.

Angelus A. Häussling, o.s.b.

5. Liturgy: Memorial of the Past and Liberation in the Present

The Church's liturgy certainly is we ourselves at worship, but the Church's liturgy, the worship of the "new, true" Israel together with that of the Israel first and enduringly chosen, is just as certainly the memorial of something past. The reference point of the memorial is the mighty deeds of God in history, datable events, not things that happened in some mythical past. They can be dated, for example, "sub Pontio Pilato," they happened at a particular time, there in the Middle East, in one of the border provinces of the vast Roman Empire. But the Church's proclamation says that these deeds of salvation are not past and gone: they retain their power today. Indeed, they are still present today because God is as radically committed to human beings now as in the past. How can that be? How is liturgy both the memorial of something past and liberation in the present?

This essay attempts to give an answer to the question thus formulated: *first,* with reference to the uniqueness of God's saving deed in Jesus Christ; *second,* with reference to the preconditions in human beings so that they may remember accurately and with engagement; *finally,* with reference to particular forms of language and celebration in which the tradition of the liturgy indicates that time has been bridged and that we today are not simply those born afterward, those who have come too late because God's saving deeds have already been accomplished.

1. The Church's great worship service, Christianity's true celebration of the new year and the renewal of the world, the Easter Vigil, asserts anew each year that salvation, peace, and freedom are not things that proceed somehow, without qualification, from the almighty God who reposes within the divine self because God, by nature, is free and therefore self-sufficient. Instead, they are deeds of liberation and preservation that God continues to work in order that all that is not God may have a share in God. Liberation from nothingness to existence in creation, liberation from the chaos of mere endurance to an orderly progression of days and years, with the Sabbath as a sign that the free human being appointed in God's stead to care for the world has a share in God's freedom, the preservation of Noah from the chaos of God's wrath, the liberation of Abraham from the monotony of the crowd to the uniqueness of covenant with YHWH, the preservation of the covenant by the calling of Moses and the rescue of the people of Israel from the dictatorship of the Egyptian superpower, by the gift of the Torah that assures a way of life in accordance with the covenant; the preservation of the covenant by the calling of prophets who repeatedly confirm Israel anew as a partner in the dialogue between YHWH and the people of God—and so continually, again and again, preservation and rescue, from the beginning of the world through the roughly two thousand years that can be counted in Israel's history before Jesus of Nazareth, to the great saving deed of God in and for Jesus himself.

Of course we have reports of other things also: God's saving acts are not always successful because people do not respond to them. They throw away their original condition, with the fatal result that they are radically unfree because they must die; more sharply still, as the terrible story of the brothers Cain and Abel teaches, with not only the possibility, but the reality that brother eliminates brother, kills him violently, that the one chosen by God is pursued by murderous hatred and struck down—and apparently God does not preserve or save him: why not? Because human freedom has triumphed over God? Where was the saving God when Cain felled his brother Abel? Only unspeakably stupid naiveté fails to see that the story of the brothers Cain and Abel is an enduring story of the human condition, and just as enduring is the human complaint: where was the saving God when Abel and the others cried out? Why did the Almighty not preserve and save them in their utmost need?

There is not only a history of salvation, but also, within it, the ongoing history of disaster.

Well, we all know that the Church's Easter celebration teaches that history arrived at its climax and turning point in Jesus of Nazareth, the last of the prophets God sent and raised up in Israel. Although he himself was God, he suffered as a human among humans, enduring the fate of Abel, of violent death as a result of betrayal and the hatred of false brothers, the cowardice of the good, and the egoistic calculation of the powerful. But what is new is that this time he did not remain subject to murder and death. It happened, as Paul says, ''in the fullness of time'' as it had at the beginning of creation, because this time God heard and saved: not by preserving Jesus from death, but, since God is mightier than death, by creating within this death itself a quality of life that breaks the domination of death, murder, and hatred, and not by making Jesus an exception, but by making him the rule, the norm, so that in every mortal and everyone moving toward death the fate of Jesus does not remain something past, but can become present reality. The bonds of death are broken: for as universally as the story of Abel occurs wherever people live, as universally as death marks the story of every human being, just as universally is it true, once the counter-story has happened, that a new form of life is awakened from death. This story of the new Abel who arises to new life, while Cain becomes the one truly dead, is what we call Easter. This event of final and enduring salvation we call, with the last Council, the Paschal mystery. What came abidingly into the world with the rescue of Jesus from death, this new quality of life that is as universal as death was before, we have called from of old the Holy Spirit: God in person, as saving gift. Pentecost is the great feast of the abiding, always new salvation, salvation with Jesus the Christ, with and in him, as long as there remains a single human being who is certainly destined to die.

But this also means that from this point on human beings are not only created in the image of God, together with Adam in the original act of salvation that was creation, but now, because God preserves and saves them, they are created anew with Jesus the Christ and thus are contemporaries of the saving deeds of God that are ever and anew something present. What greater thing can be said of human beings: with Jesus of Nazareth, the Christ, they are the continual recipients and contemporaries of God's acts of salvation.

2. But human freedom remains. People can make themselves blind and refuse to acknowledge their situation. Their memory of the model of salvation, this Jesus of Nazareth, as preserved in the Gospels and proclaimed by the Church throughout the generations, can be suppressed and even denied. In fact, as we all know, each person's memory and power of recollection is different. We choose what we want to remember. The inconvenient things we put aside, along with everything we judge less important because not immediately useful. Psychology has made some interesting studies of selective memory, that is, the things people remember. Let me refer briefly to this by quoting Friedrich Nietzsche: " 'I have done that,' says my memory. 'I cannot have done that,' says my pride, and remains inexorable. Eventually—memory yields."[1]

The memory we are speaking of first requires the courage to affirm oneself as a limited, fallible human being in need of crucial assistance because subject to sin and death. It requires the repentance to which John the Baptizer called human beings; it needs the faith Jesus of Nazareth demands. These are also the preconditions that the free human being must produce: there can be no *memoria* of the deeds of salvation without repentance, without true humility, without faith. Otherwise people would not be free and God would not be all-powerful. There can be no sacrament without faith, no fes-

---

[1] Friedrich Nietzsche, *Beyond Good and Evil*, part 4, epigram 68. Quoted from the translation by Walter Kaufmann (New York: Vintage/Random House, 1966) 80. See also Sigmund Freud, *Zur Psychopathologie des Alltagslebens* (Frankfurt a. M., 1974) 119. Quoted also in M. Osterland, "Die Mythologisierung des Lebenslaufs. Zur Problematik des Erinnerns," in: Martin Baethge and Wolfgang Essbach, eds., *Soziologie: Entdeckungen im Alltäglichen. Hans Paul Bahrdt Festschrift zu seinem 65. Geburtstag* (Frankfurt and New York, 1983) 279–90, at 284, with n. 22 on 289.

tal celebration, no Easter and Pentecost without the Quad-ragesima of the exercise of faith.

3. But how can human beings "remember" the saving deeds of God in Jesus the Christ? This is not simply "think-ing about" (as, I believe, the German common translation [*Einheitsübersetzung*] of the Bible unfortunately represents the biblical idea of "remembering" throughout). It is not a men-tal process that goes on behind the eyebrows. It has a linguis-tic form and must express in words the fact that people who remember have become something different; they can and must understand themselves as different. They must be able to interpret themselves in terms of what they remember and what the memory effects in them. Worship in Israel found a linguistic form for this, and it has been carried forward with-out interruption in the Church's liturgy. I will give an academic description for this form: self-definition by imitative assump-tion of the roles of the leading historical figures of the norma-tive era of salvation through situative identity.

3.1. What does that mean? As I have said, we are contem-poraries of God's saving deeds. Historical contemporaries say and acknowledge what they experience. What do the later ones do, what do we do, if in the reality of the sacraments we are also contemporaries? What do people do who have entered a phase displacement in which the witnesses of history are no longer alive, and yet the events of previous history have not ceased to be reality? They, the later ones, identify themselves as contemporaries, which they are through the power of sacramental reality; they do so by using textual quotations to put themselves in the roles of the historical contemporaries: as they were, so are we. Or, because the situation is the same—that of human disaster and divine acts of salvation—I redis-cover myself, in self-interpretation, in those who at that time were authentic witnesses and gave their witness in words. When I adopt their testimony as my own, I find myself.

Let me give a very simple example that every reader has already practiced many times, but probably never thought about: what happens when a Christian prays the Lord's prayer, the Our Father? Luke's Gospel tells us that, being touched by Jesus' example and wanting to pray in imitation of him as a sign of discipleship, the disciples of Rabbi Jesus ask for a prayer, and Jesus gives them one that is his and theirs (Luke 11:1-4; cf. Matt 6:9-13), and that from then on Jesus' disciples practice it as their own prayer. What does anyone do who prays the Our Father as her or his own? It is not merely the repetition of a profound formula that has been retained because its statement is more adequate than any other, or because it is preserved in the Gospel.

What the one praying does is first of all to demonstrate that she or he is a disciple of Jesus committed to obedience and therefore a contemporary of the Twelve and hence of the normative and thus enduring era of salvation because like them she or he petitions the Lord and practices the Lord's response as something binding. Asking and praying like the apostles and with them, such a one learns, in practicing the Gospel commands, to interpret her- or himself as a contemporary of Jesus. Hence it is not surprising that the first known command for the daily practice of prayer in Christianity is: "You should pray in this way three times a day!" (*Didache* [late 1st c.] 8.3).

The Gospels offer us two versions of the text, a longer one in Matthew (and in the *Didache* just mentioned) and a shorter one in Luke. Quite apart from the question of exegetes' interpretation of the history of the text in detail, this double tradition means that the primitive Church was not interested in a sacred formula, but in the state of contemporaneity affirmed in asking, hearing, obeying, and praying like the apostles, which is conveyed by means of the Lord's prayer. This identification of roles through quotation defines Christians who remain contemporary with God's saving deeds.

Once we have been made aware of this form of language, other examples quickly come to mind. It was customary in the synagogue liturgy to define the theological locus of divine worship and of the change in the situation of those celebrating, which happened in the worship service, by means of a quotation from the sixth chapter of Isaiah. Isaiah was about twenty-five years old when, ca. 740 B.C.E., he was called to prophesy. In his vision he sees YHWH enthroned above the Temple, surrounded by the heavenly court, and perceives how they preserve their very existence from the scorching holiness of YHWH: the seraphim call out to one another unceasingly, with a power that shakes the foundations of the Temple, what they see and confess: YHWH is holy (6:1-4). This confession of YHWH by the heavenly court is taken up by the community of God as its own confession, quoting the book of the prophet.

We know it in our own familiar liturgy as well, in the great prayer at every Eucharistic celebration. This is not because the prophet's account yields a magnificent hymn, but because by citing the prophet's role the liturgical community defines itself: it now stands in the place of the seraphim: the locus of their worship is in heaven, in the presence of God; heaven and earth are united, and those who celebrate in this community are no longer sinful people estranged from God, but, like the prophet, they are those who see God; like the seraphim, they are those who confess God; as human beings in time they are contemporary with God's saving actions and may define themselves as such by this citation of role—not in an abstract instruction that produces nothing but boredom and is never really persuasive, but through participation in a history that God never ceases to create, as long as human beings exist.

It is striking, although we cannot discuss the reasons for it in detail here, that the first two chapters of the Gospel of Luke define their speaker. The hymn of the angels over the shepherds' field in Bethlehem (2:14) forms the opening of an old church hymn constructed of acclamations that derives its name, ''Gloria,'' from the angels' song (first attested in the *Apostolic Constitutions* 7.47 [4th c.]), and that still has a secure place in the Church's worship. The quotation, like that from Isaiah 6, defines the locus of worship and the new role of the hymn singers: where the Church praises God, God is present, and those who give praise in faith are situated in the community of God's life.

Another place for the identification of roles through quotation is the reading of the Gospel in the worship services of morning and evening prayer, which—following a general rule of liturgical development—very quickly fixed on the canticles sung in the first two chapters of Luke's Gospel by Zechariah, Mary, and Simeon. Their psalmodic form, the deep conviction of the speakers, and the intensity of the original situation within the history of salvation are incomparably apt for identification. We have testimony going back to the sixth century that, by the use of the *Magnificat* in the great evening prayer (Vespers), of the *Nunc dimittis* in the prayer before going to rest (Compline), and of the *Benedictus* at morning prayer (Lauds), those praying have identified themselves as the contemporaries of those saving deeds whose accomplishment is signified for them through the ages in the figures of the mother of Jesus, the priest of the Jerusalem Temple and father of the last prophet before Jesus, and the aged Simeon whose lifelong desire has now been fulfilled.

But the use of the psalms in worship represents the most comprehensive definition through identification of roles. The tradition of the people of God regarded them as compositions by King David, the one chosen by God and called to be the leader of divine praise, but also a sinful human being who had been pardoned through sorrow and repentance. If I am correct, there is no other reason to justify such an intensive use of the psalms in the Church's liturgy if not that we are to have pointed out to us the possibility of seeing ourselves reflected in the speaker of the psalms, in the same situation of disaster and salvation, and thereby of understanding ourselves. We know from the tradition of the liturgy of the hours that we should begin our day with Psalm 51(50), introduced as a biographical psalm of David after deep sinfulness and pardon (cf. 51[50]:1-2). (A quotation from 51[50]:17 opens the first hour of daily prayer, and the whole psalm is the first unit in the morning office; this is still the case in the post-conciliar *Liturgia horarum* of 1971, in Lauds of every Friday.)

Beyond this, the psalms express the fundamental and abiding experiences of distance from God, of need, of the inability to understand what God does and does not do, with our reactions to these things: complaint, despairing cries in the depths of powerlessness, and even cursing (although these last formulae were eliminated from the liturgical texts by Pope Paul VI). These are reactions that, bucking the trend to liturgical perfection, can still be expressed only here: and that, indeed, must find expression in people's worship of God, simply because they, too, are the truth of our existence.

Of course, it is not only David whom we quote in the psalms when we identify there our situation of salvation from disaster. It is also Jesus himself, whose word and role we here adopt.

According to the Gospels, it was by means of the psalms that the Lord himself, when he was dying on the cross, embraced his terrible death endured as a guiltless victim of violence. While dying, Jesus prayed Psalm 22(21): "My God, my God, why have you forsaken me?" (Mark 15:34; Matt 27:46 = Ps 22:2; in ancient literary custom, the citation of the beginning of a text refers to the text as a whole). It is an expression of the most extreme alienation from God, and whoever suffers it at any time enters into the role of Jesus the crucified, identifying with him in his redeeming action, and then praising with him the salvation of which the psalm speaks in the latter part of its text. For the evangelist Luke, it appears, the alienation from God expressed by this psalm was too severe; he reports instead that in his death Jesus spoke the usual evening prayer of a pious Israelite, the psalm verse "into your hand I commit my spirit," prefacing it with Jesus' typical address to God: "Abba, Father" (Ps 31[30]:5, at Luke 23:46). Since then, praying the psalms has not been the uttering of some pious statements or other before God, but Christians' identification with the role of their Christ, beginning with Stephen, who, like Jesus, dies praying a psalm (Acts 7:59), and continuing to the final cry of the last believers in Christ in the unavoidable distress before the final coming of the Lord.

3.2. This description of a literary stylistic device in the liturgy cannot stand without an added remark on the shift that occurred in the Middle Ages. At that time a new experience of symbol and image, and a different conception of time and history, led thinking away from the traditional idea of self-definition through identification in the assumption of roles to a depiction through imagery, and from the real symbolism of the sacrament that transforms the baptized who celebrate the Eucharist in a fundamental way, beyond any rational understanding, to an imitative role-play that draws on the scenes of the past and opens the people's disposition to the profundity of the experience. To give another example, let us consider this time the other prayer text that is part of the basic fund of Christian prayers, the Hail Mary.

This text describes a fixed set of scenes: first it quotes the greeting of the archangel Gabriel to Mary as reported by the Gospel of Luke (1:28); then the speaker (or imitator) changes roles and quotes the words of greeting spoken by Mary's cousin, Elizabeth, to her (1:42). In this way, the sacred history is played out before the speaker. In the third part of the text, the most recent, originating in the fifteenth century and given its definitive formulation in the breviary of Pope Pius V (1568), those praying speak for themselves and draw the moral application from what has been illustrated in the drama: acknowledging that they are sinners and requesting the aid of this woman who in the fullness of the time of salvation was so uniquely graced: "Holy Mary, Mother of God, pray for us sinners, now and at the hour of our death." Those who take the Our Father as their own text interpret themselves, in the citation, according to their role as Christians: obedient disciples of Jesus just like the apostles. But those who pray the Hail Mary immerse themselves meditatively in sacred history, are touched in their emotions and ask that this figure from the era of salvation would turn as advocate to them, the poor and suffering, so that when the time of salvation begins for them God's mercy may be available to them.

The Middle Ages were zealous and devoted in exposing the mysteries of faith by means of sacred drama, but at the same time they often created an unbridgeable distance between the saving events of past time, recalled in the liturgical *memoria,* and the situation of those born afterward, who present themselves in the sacred drama. As far as we know the sacred drama began with a depiction of the women going to the tomb on Easter Sunday morning. The medieval Easter play still survives in the second part of the sequence for the Mass of Easter Sunday, the "Victimae paschali laudes" by Wipo, the court chaplain of Emperor Conrad II, dating from the first half of the eleventh century, and included also in the post-conciliar missal. More critical for the spirituality of Catholic Christianity was the fact that the Middle Ages also understood the Mass itself as an imitative drama of the passion of Jesus, in which ultimately the priest was allotted the role of the Lord himself, since within the Eucharistic prayer he speaks the Lord's words over the bread and wine as his own, in the first person. It did not bother the Middle Ages at all that, as phenotype, the ritual of the Mass scarcely suggested anything like a drama of the passion story. For the mentality of the time, imitative drama was the proper means for self-identification in light of God's saving deeds, having the advantage of subjective feeling, but the danger of oversimplification, of failing to perceive the reality proper to the sacrament, namely, the presence of the effects of salvation that is unconfined by time, and of failing to realize the turning point in history for which Easter and Pentecost stand. Increasingly it was no longer the resurrection of the Lord and the presence of his Spirit that constituted the source of the Church's life.

Here the baroque era, which both continued and even exceeded the Middle Ages in this respect, reveals in a remarkable way the profound engagement of individuals as a result of their being directed into the roles of participants and imitators in deep and genuine understanding of the Gospel. One example is the phenomenon of pilgrimage to the scourged Savior in Wies, which emerged spontaneously in the eighteenth century and rapidly reached an amazing magnitude. The religious image of the Savior, bound to the scourging post to which people's sins had chained him, and there suffering patiently for our sake, gave Christians, themselves plagued by so many troubles, the possibility not only of edifying themselves through the example of Jesus, but of identifying with Jesus in their suffering, imitating him as a model of patience, following him and in this sacred play becoming convinced and convincing participants with him. In fact, we are still surprised today by the spontaneity and genuineness of the numerous testimonials in the votive images and memorials in the church at Wies, extending over two centuries to the present time, as expressions of gratitude to the Lord, that unsurpassable figure of identification, for consolation received.

No one can deny the religious value of such things, and we are made to ask ourselves with shame whether the Church today knows how to offer those in need any spiritual aid that is similar in its intensity. However, we may ask whether, in this consolation of suffering together with the Savior, the Lord's resurrection and the presence of his saving deeds that effects a fundamental change in our circumstances do not so recede into the background that the good news of the victory over death, the gift of the Spirit, and the vocation of Christians to be contemporaries of Jesus the Christ remain so distant that they no longer affect pious minds and, as a result, are unable to explode the constriction brought about by a Gothic and baroque mentality with its concentration on subjective feeling, so as to broaden our minds to the duty to turn to the world and, with Christ, to change it.

4. The era and the environment in which God's almighty providence has placed us, the Christians of the North Atlantic societies at the end of the twentieth century, no longer furnish us with support in our duty to pray to God, to remember God's mighty deeds, and to praise God's greatness. We accomplish our task only with difficulty; it has become a heavy burden to us. It is in just such a situation that a reference to the memorial of the past and the way in which the ancient Church made liberation a present reality in every age is so important. For even in an environment of actual or prescribed atheism the ancient, simple, modest form for discovering and defining oneself as a Christian remains open to everyone, even to children, when we, like Christians in the second and subsequent generations, learn to enter salvation history by means of role imitation—our own salvation history, to which we, despite the progress of time, have become and remained contemporaries. Today God still cares for human beings, and God is as close to us in effecting the deeds of salvation as to others in the past. But our brothers and sisters in faith from the ancient Church have left us in the liturgy a stylistic form that, if we use it, can still tell us today that we are not latecomers, but are and always will be the contemporaries of Jesus the Christ.

Klemens Richter

6. Liturgical Reform
as the Means for Church Renewal*

I. Liturgy as "Dangerous Memory" in the World and in the Church

Johann Baptist Metz understands the *memoria* of the suffering, death, and resurrection of Jesus Christ as a "dangerous memory." In this *memoria*, the most basic form of expression of Christian faith, we recall the testament of Christ's love and thereby we remember that this *memoria* contains a particular anticipation of the future as the future of the hopeless, the broken, and the oppressed. This memorial is both a dangerous and a liberating memory because it threatens the present and calls it into question; because, in fact, this memorial "compels Christians constantly to change themselves so that they are able to take this future into account."[1]

We will not at this point pursue the question why Metz, the systematic theologian, despite all his impressive admonitions to locate this *memoria* at the center of Christian faith and action, does not get around to speaking about the liturgy, which effects this *memoria* in celebration, and which is the fore-

---

* This essay appeared in a slightly different form in Klemens Richter, ed., *Das Konzil war erst der Anfang. Die Bedeutung des II. Vatikanums für Theologie und Kirche* (Mainz, 1991) 53–74.

[1] Johann Baptist Metz, *Faith in History and Society, Toward a Practical Fundamental Theology,* translated by David Smith (New York: Crossroad, 1980) 90.

most locus of memory of God's dealings with God's people.[2] But his central thesis, according to which "the Church must understand and justify itself as the public witness and bearer of the tradition of a dangerous memory of freedom in the 'systems' of our emancipative society,"[3] is ultimately founded on liturgical celebration.

When he asks whether Christianity has been a historical failure and whether the Church, as institutional vehicle of that Christianity and its *memoria*, is historically passé; when he says that the dangerous memory is extinguished and eschatological recollection is exhausted, these must also be understood as challenging the liturgy and as questioning whether our memorial celebration of the death and resurrection of our Lord is such as to change consciousness and structures. And that is also a question about the structures of Church and congregation, ultimately a challenge to their own self-understanding.

Memoria or *anamnesis* is the making present in celebration of a historical event of salvation, whereby the event remains a past event in the liturgical action, but is actualized in the present and thus exercises a concrete effect. The memorial of God's saving action in Jesus Christ has always, from the very beginning, initiated an action, as the New Testament assures us (cf., among other passages, Acts 10:4, 31; Rom 1:5; Gal 2:10).

The subject of the liturgical memorial is God's plan of salvation, which encompasses past, present, and future until the eschaton, and which, for Christians, had its culmination in Jesus. He, Jesus Christ, is the primary actor in the liturgy, the one who draws the community into his action. In their actions he gives a visible form to his presence. His priestly office endures in the actions of the community, which is therefore the secondary subject of the liturgical memorial celebration.

The way in which the congregation exercises its role will shape its own self-understanding and its structure as a com-

---

[2] Cf. Angelus A. Häussling, "Liturgiewissenschaft zwei Jahrzehnte nach Konzilsbeginn. Eine Umschau im deutschen Sprachgebiet," *ALW* 24 (1982): 11; also Klemens Richter, "Die Liturgie—zentrales Thema der Theologie," in *idem*, ed., *Liturgie—ein vergessens Thema der Theologie?* QB 107 (Freiburg, 2d ed. 1987) 21–22.

[3] *Faith in History and Society*, 89–90.

munity: whether it really understands itself as the subject of the liturgy or delegates the action almost entirely to the priest, as we know was the case in the West for almost a millennium. The image and understanding of Church underlying a situation in which the ability to celebrate liturgy is attributed only to ordained officials is different from that which is operative where the community as a whole understands itself as responsible for liturgical celebration.

To that extent, then, the understanding of liturgy newly shaped by Vatican II may probably be described as a "dangerous memory" for the Church and the community's self-understanding; and to that extent the liturgical *memoria* has substantial consequences for a renewal of the Church.

II. The Relationship of Church and Liturgy

The very first sentence of the conciliar document makes it clear that Vatican II aimed at a comprehensive renewal of the Church: an intensification of Christian life, adjustment of "those observances which are open to adaptation" to the requirements of our times, the promotion of the unity of all Christians—and for that reason alone, a "renewal of the liturgy" was also necessary.[4] But even a scant three decades after the publication of the constitution *Sacrosanctum concilium* on 4 December 1963, we are slowly becoming aware that it can only be understood against the background of a renewed ecclesiology. Quite rightly an evangelical theologian has written, in a commentary on the apostolic letter *Vicesimus quintus annus* of John Paul II on the twenty-fifth anniversary of the Constitution on the Liturgy,[5] "We must admit that no decision has had such immediate consequences for the spiritual life of congregations as the reform of the liturgy. Ecclesiology and liturgy are inseparable."[6] The Pope indicates in the second

---

[4] *SC* 1.

[5] The Latin text is in *Osservatore Romano* 114, 14 May 1989. For the English translation, see *Origins* 19 (1989/90) 17ff.

[6] Friedemann Merkel, "Die römische Liturgie—25 Jahre nach der Reform," *Materialdienst des Konfessionskundlichen Instituts Bensheim* 41 (1990) 1, 3–7, at 3.

paragraph of his letter, quoting himself, that in the liturgy constitution "the substance of that ecclesiological doctrine that would later be put before the conciliar assembly is already evident."[7] It anticipated the dogmatic constitution *Lumen gentium*. And in the fourth paragraph he clearly indicates that he is aware of the unbreakable connection between liturgical reform and Church reform: "Together with the biblical renewal, the ecumenical movement, the missionary impetus, and ecclesiological research, the reform of the liturgy was to contribute to the overall renewal of the church. I drew attention to this in the letter *Dominicae cenae:* 'A very close and organic bond exists between the renewal of the liturgy and the renewal of the whole life of the church.' "[8]

"Vatican II set itself against a static-institutional concept of the Church by accenting the ecclesiologies of community, of the people of God, and of sacrament, thereby correcting a number of earlier, one-sided views. . . . These sketch a historical, dynamic image of the Church as process. . . ."[9] The Council "repeatedly and urgently emphasized, first of all in the Constitution on the Liturgy (2), the ancient truth, first mentioned in Scripture (cf. 1 Cor 10:17; Acts 2:42), and developed especially by Ignatius of Antioch, Augustine, Leo the Great, and Thomas Aquinas, that the Church is built up by the celebration of the Eucharist and manifests itself primarily in that celebration."[10] Thus we can speak of a Eucharistic ecclesiology even in Western theology today,[11] an ecclesiology

---

[7] Address to the participants in the Congress of Presidents and Secretaries of National Liturgy Commissions, 27 October 1984, no. 1: *Insegnamenti* 7/2 (1984) 1049.

[8] Letter "Dominicae Cenae," 24 February 1980, 13: *AAS* 72 (1980) 146.

[9] Stefan Rau, *Die Feiern der Gemeinden und das Recht der Kirche. Zu Aufgabe, Form und Ebenen liturgischer Gesetzgebung in der katholischen Kirche.* MThA 12 (Altenberge, 1990) 294. Cf. here the section "Der ekklesiologische Neuansatz des II. Vatikanischen Konzils [The new ecclesiological initiative of Vatican II]" 274–94, which includes the more recent literature on the subject.

[10] Emil J. Lengeling, "Eucharistiefeier und Pfarrgemeinde. Aufgaben nach dem Konzil," in: Adolf Exeler, ed., *Die neue Gemeinde* (Mainz, 1967) 136–66, at 158.

[11] Cf. *inter alia*, Anton Thaler, *Gemeinde und Eucharistie. Grundlegung*

that sees itself in terms of the liturgical celebrations of individual congregations and constructs Church from that starting point.

Because no other expression of the Church's life is such a clear statement of ecclesial identity as the liturgy, and "no other action of the Church can match its claim to efficacy, nor equal the degree of it,"[12] with the celebration of the Eucharist being called the "fount and apex of the whole Christian life,"[13] and because, therefore, divine worship is a mirror of the whole life of the Church, since it presents the real symbol of the Church itself, it must necessarily reflect actual conditions in the Church, and be an expression of its faith and of its life. It is evident from history that every great conflict within the Church has also brought about differences in the liturgy. Different accents in the interpretation of faith require different worship services because faith and the expression of faith in liturgy cannot be separated. The development toward a Roman, Latin clergy in the Middle Ages was connected with a view of the Church as structured from the top down, for at that time the celebration of the liturgy was connected with the clerics, who alone were capable of liturgical action. Even the canon law that was in force until quite recently asserted that all actions in the worship service could only be "performed by persons legitimately designated,"[14] even though the ancient Church understood liturgy as the worship of a congregation, though obviously not without its presider.

One result of this development was that the celebration of the Eucharist, the memorial of Christ's paschal mystery, was no longer the center of believers' devotion, but was replaced by other forms of piety drawn from private devotional life and therefore secondary. In the Eucharist itself it was no longer the celebration as a whole that was its center, but the elevation after the consecration, the adoration of the sacred host, while the Lord's supper itself, instituted by the Lord with the

---

einer eucharistischen Ekklesiologie. Praktische Theologie im Dialog 2 (Fribourg, 1988).

[12] *SC* 7.

[13] *LG* 11.

[14] *CIC* 1917, canon 1256.

words, "do this in remembrance of me," was scarcely received more than once a year.

The principle that the image of the Church and its understanding of liturgy must correspond is as valid for the Reformation as for the traditionalist movement in the Western industrialized countries in recent years. Those who want the so-called Tridentine Mass at least have a clear conception of Church: ordered in a unified fashion from top to bottom, with the cleric as the *vir dei*, the holy man of God, without whom the laity can receive scarcely any share in the grace mediated by the sacraments, which the cleric controls. According to the pastoral sociologist Paul M. Zulehner,[15] this corresponds to the pastoral concept of the village churches of the past: an authoritarian, directive, and external pastoral care. It is only logical, then, that Archbishop Marcel Lefebvre should lead a backward march toward the Middle Ages and thus avoid the question of how, in this secularized society, a life oriented to the Gospel is possible outside a self-created ghetto. This example makes the unbreakable bond between liturgy and ecclesiology dramatically obvious: those who reject liturgical reform as a whole must also disagree with the whole conciliar reform of the Church, and must logically reject all of Vatican II.

> If the Council had defined the Church as a closed society, liturgical reform would be simple: the Church could be like a sect, in which a close, familiar group practices a traditional ritual whose cultic-historical and preservationist value cannot be challenged. Perfecting such a ritual and purifying it of anything differing from the "ancient, traditional norms of the holy ancestors" could then be called liturgical reform, as in fact has long been our custom. But the Second Vatican Council saw the Church quite differently; it is supposed to respond to the paradigm shifts of history. The Council thus entrusted the Church with "liturgical reform," as it understood it, as an enduring and never finished task, without giving thought to the unforeseeable difficulties this involves.

---

[15] On this, see Klemens Richter, "Liturgie und Seelsorge in der katholischen Kirche seit Beginn des 20. Jahrhunderts," in: Kaspar Elm and Hans Dietrich Loock, ed., *Seelsorge und Diakonie in Berlin* (Berlin and New York, 1990) 585–608, at 603.

It appears (presupposing that the Church remains true to the Council) that liturgy reform to this point has been nothing but a prelude.[16]

However, we cannot overlook the fact that such fidelity is not always practiced, and especially not in Rome. Thus we must surely call it "a mockery of the Council"[17] when the curial Cardinal Augustin Mayer, O.S.B., ordains priests using the medieval Tridentine ritual, as he did in 1988. We can only agree with Peter Hünermann's remark on the context as a whole: "I know of no historical parallel for such a suspension of the decisions of a legitimate Council."[18] If we compare this proceeding with the papal letter, the question arises whether in Rome—to adapt the saying—the center does not know what the right is doing.

III. Vatican II: "The End of the Liturgical Middle Ages"

˙My predecessor in the chair of liturgical studies in Münster, Emil J. Lengeling, who participated in the normative renewal of worship, both on a global level and in the German-speaking world, to an extent scarcely equaled by any other German theologian, saw the publication of the Constitution on the Liturgy as the "end of the liturgical Middle Ages." The Constitution not only concludes the post-Tridentine period, but in its aims it connects with many things that had been lost or, in part, had already vanished when the Church entered the German regions. The Council is not only concerned to eliminate the post-Tridentine rigidity: this reform is meant to take courageously in hand what, for a variety of historical (cultural as well as political) reasons, had been neglected much earlier within the Western Church."[19]

[16] Angelus A. Häußling, "Liturgiereform. Materialien zu einem neuen Thema der Liturgiewissenschaft," *ALW* 31 (1989) 1–32, at 30.

[17] *Ibid.*, 32 n. 87. Cf. *Herder Korrespondenz* 43 (1989) 43–44.

[18] Peter Hünermann, "Droht eine dritte Modernismuskrise?" *Herder Korrespondenz* 43 (1989) 130–35, at 133.

[19] Reprinted in Emil J. Lengeling, *Liturgie—Dialog zwischen Gott und Mensch,* edited by Klemens Richter (Altenberge, 2d ed. 1991) 13–14.

That a process undertaken in such comprehensive scope[20] should not go forward without pain, and that a variety of problem areas would arise, is really a matter of course. In any case, history teaches us that every Council was followed by a more or less intensive phase of appropriation of its decisions, a process of reception or non-reception. Certainly, the movement initiated by the Constitution on the Liturgy has in the meantime become irreversible as a whole. But it is by no means certain that the goals of the reform have really been achieved in the fullest sense. Such a project is the task of a century, and even today, alongside many positive aspects, we can detect a variety of darker results.

Therefore it is indeed welcome that, in fact, all the evaluations of the liturgical reform that have appeared in honor of the twentieth and twenty-fifth anniversaries[21] have declined to break forth in a one-sided and euphoric chorus of jubilation, but instead indicate the deficiencies alongside the happy achievements, and formulate tasks for the future. The goal of the Constitution on the Liturgy was, in fact, not a reform of the liturgy alone, but its concern was and is "to intensify the daily growth of Catholics in Christian living; to make more responsive to the requirements of our times those Church observances which are open to adaptation; to nurture whatever can contribute to the unity of all who believe in Christ. . . ."[22] It is thus a matter, as the German-speaking bishops wrote at the time,

> of renewal and strengthening of religious life through liturgical renewal; so that we and our congregations, amidst all the dangers that today threaten the faith of every Christian,

---

[20] Cf. Annibale Bugnini, *Die Liturgiereform 1948–1975. Zeugnis und Testament*, edited by Johannes Wagner (Freiburg, 1988).

[21] Cf., *inter alia*, Emil J. Lengeling , "Zum 20. Jahrestag der Liturgiekonstitution," *LJ* 34 (1984) 114–24; Reiner Kaczynski, "20 Jahre Liturgiereform, Rückschau und Ausblick," *MThZ* 35 (1985) 52–66; Theodor Maas-Ewerd, ed., *Lebt unser Gottesdienst? Die bleibende Aufgabe der Liturgiereform*. Festschrift for Bruno Kleinheyer (Freiburg, 1988); Hansjakob Becker, Bernd J. Hilberath, and Ulrich Willers, ed., *Gottesdienst—Kirche—Gesellschaft. Standortbestimmungen nach 25. Jahren Liturgiereform*. Pietas liturgica 5 (St. Ottilien, 1991).

[22] *SC* 1.

may find the way to the risen Lord who is present and active in the liturgy. . . .[23]

Because the liturgy is a celebration of faith, the continual renewal of this celebration is an essential task of Christian communities. When

> the Decree on Ecumenism says of the Church, in Article 6, that it is called to "that continual reformation of which [it] always has need, insofar as [it] is an institution of [human beings] here on earth," and therefore . . . "if the influence of events or of the times has led to deficiencies in conduct, in Church discipline, or even in the formulation of doctrine . . . these should be appropriately rectified at the proper moment," the same is true of the liturgy.[24]

Renewal of worship is therefore an ongoing process, but it is only possible under conditions of constant attention and readiness to change. Hence the Munich liturgist Reiner Kaczynski could write, in a provisional appraisal:

> Those who today, twenty-five years after the publication of the Constitution on the Liturgy ask, whether this central goal of Church renewal has been attained will have to admit that it has no more been achieved than after ten, fifteen, or twenty years, and no less than it will have been attained after fifty years; for an *ecclesia semper reformanda* requires a *liturgia semper reformanda*. The question is more properly whether we are ready for a renewal of worship, and through it a renewal of the Church, that will still be necessary twenty-five years in the future, or whether we are content with the condition of what we have achieved, with its differences from congregation to congregation, and do not even take opposing action when old abuses that we thought had been done away with reappear, or when new ones are introduced.[25]

[23] Pastoral letter of the German-speaking bishops to their clergy, 18 February 1964, in Emil J. Lengeling, *Die Konstitution des Zweiten Vatikanischen Konzils über die heilige Liturgie. Lat.-dt. Text mit Kommentar.* Series Lebendiger Gottesdienst 5/6 (Münster, 2d ed. 1965) 7*–12*, at 9*.

[24] Vatican Council II, *Decree on Ecumenism* 6. See also Emil J. Lengeling, "Zum 20. Jahrestag," (see n. 21 above) 123.

[25] Reiner Kaczynski, "Erneuerung der Kirche durch den Gottesdienst," in: *Lebt unser Gottesdienst?* (see n. 21 above) 15–16.

Here we should also mention ungrasped opportunities,[26] and from two points of view: on the one hand, we should recognize the things that have been neglected in our own country. Balthasar Fischer has compared the process of liturgical renewal to a magnificent cathedral which is suddenly discovered to be lacking a foundation. The foundation is the spirit of reform, the theological basis; anyone who wanted to slavishly follow the minutiae of the new liturgical books in the way that was demanded by the preconciliar liturgy would not have grasped the sense of the reform. On the other hand, the dynamics of the reform process itself have raised new questions that could not even be envisioned a quarter of a century ago, but that today call for new answers.

We can speak of an end to the liturgical Middle Ages because the liturgical reform has again made obvious some utterly original principles of a Christian understanding of liturgy that had received too little attention over the course of time. The liturgical movement was a consequence of the biblical movement. The effort to reorient Christian life more strongly to the origins of Christian community necessarily led to the question of the extent to which a Mass following the rules of the 1570 Missal of Pius V bore any resemblance to the primitive community's celebration of the Lord's supper. Within such a Mass, lasting thirty minutes, the celebrant was required "to genuflect every two minutes, make the sign of the cross every thirty-five seconds, kiss the altar every three minutes: altogether sixteen genuflections, fifty-two signs of the cross, and ten altar-kissings. Was that wrong? It is a question without an answer."[27] But we can scarcely blame those to whom this does not look like an adequate expression of what took place in that room at the Last Supper.

The reform therefore attempted, while preserving the essential elements of the tradition, at least to recover the basic struc-

---

[26] On this, cf. Klemens Richter, "Nicht genutzte Chancen der Liturgiereform," in: Hubert Ritt, ed., *Auferstehung. Ostern bis Pfingsten. Gottes Volk, Bibel und Liturgie im Leben der Gemeinde. Lesejahr C 4* (Stuttgart, 1989) 105–18.

[27] Heinrich Rennings, "Aus Treue zur Tradition: Reform der Liturgie," *Liturgiereform im Streit der Meinungen.* Studien und Berichte der Katholischen Akademie in Bayern 42 (Würzburg, 1968) 147–61, at 153.

ture of liturgical celebration as manifested by its beginnings. Incidentally, that was also the intention of the Council of Trent, which, however, because of a lack of the necessary scholarship, was unable to trace the development of the liturgy farther back than the twelfth century. One may certainly suppose that the new Missal of Paul VI of 1970 is approximately what people hoped to achieve four hundred years ago: essentially a collection of texts drawn from the whole tradition, while— and this is a criticism of the whole reform that deserves to be taken seriously—less attention was paid to the situation of the community today. We may with good reason say that it is more or less the structures of late antiquity or the early medieval Church that constitute the foundation of the new order.

However, we can speak of an end to the liturgical Middle Ages because the reform has brought about a decisive paradigm shift or, in other words, a critical change in perspective.[28] This can best be seen, independently of all individual aspects of the reform, in two directly connected fields. On the one hand, there is the replacement of a static by a dynamic conception of liturgy, and on the other hand, the liturgy is no longer understood simply as a celebration *for* the community, but as a celebration *of* the faith of the community.

IV. From a Static to a Dynamic Liturgy

Probably few are aware that, even among those in our communities who regularly participate in liturgical celebrations, there is a kind of deficit in contemporaneity, a strongly contradictory notion of liturgy and Church. On the one hand, there are those who are still tied to a preconciliar way of thinking, who at least internally, for whatever reasons, have not made the shift to a conciliar theology—those, that is, whose mentality remains largely unchanged and who go primarily to fulfill their obligation, as we learned to do before the Council, and who therefore expect to have grace dispensed to them through the Mass in a reasonable length of time, and protest if it lasts longer than forty-five minutes; for whom it is not the Eucharis-

[28] Cf. Angelus A. Häußling, "Nachkonziliare Paradigmenwechsel und das Schicksal der Liturgiereform," *ThG* 32 (1989) 243–54.

tic celebration itself, but its results that are important, meaning thereby the consecration and the Eucharistic species,
whereas what is really at stake is the consecration (i.e., the
transformation) of the community through communion with
the body and blood of the Lord. On the other side are those
for whom this kind of grace-dispensing mentality has come
to seem almost blasphemous, and who are alienated by such
an accomplishment-oriented view of worship. These extremes
illustrate the contrast between a more static and a more dynamic conception of liturgy.

Liturgy has nothing to do with the accomplishment of something or the performance of some obligation before God. It is,
in the first place, not a matter of a cultic ritual owed to God,
and certainly not a negotiation with a God who demands certain services from human beings that can then be rewarded.
The latter conception played an important role in the Middle
Ages in light of people's anxiety over sin and judgment. But
worship is first of all a celebration of faith in which God, the
creator and redeemer, is praised without any ulterior motive—
that is, without any idea of gaining anything thereby. An Afri-
can priest thought he was encountering a completely different faith when he was confronted with the time limits of our
Sunday worship services. He could not discern from the appearance or from the brevity of our celebration of the Mass that
this is supposed to be the center of our lives. And he asked
whether we also behave so coldly when we celebrate with our
friends, and shove our guests out the door after scarcely an
hour has passed. This should certainly give us pause for
thought; it is a challenge to our conception of worship and a
question to be pondered: what, in fact, the liturgy means for us.

Here two different viewpoints in our communities collide.
In this respect, the extreme ideas may be seen as corresponding to a purely vertical cultic worship and a purely horizontal
get-together. But the two belong together, for in the liturgy
also the way to God is through other people. It is not some
individualistic salvational function to fulfill the slogan ''save
your soul.'' There can be no such thing as a private Mass.

The replacement of a centuries-old static conception of liturgy by a dynamic one can probably be illustrated most clearly
by considering the succession of modes of presence of Jesus

Christ in the celebrating community, as repeatedly described in the post-conciliar documents. Thus in Article 7 of the General Instruction of the Roman Missal we read that ". . . at the celebration of Mass, . . . Christ is really present to the assembly gathered in his name; he is present in the person of the minister, in his own word, and indeed substantially and permanently under the Eucharistic elements."[29] Thus the Eucharistic celebration is no longer described exclusively in terms of the Eucharistic gifts, that is, in terms of a presence of the Lord in the Eucharistic species that is to be understood primarily in static terms. Instead, it is seen as a process: the Lord is first of all present in those assembled, in accordance with his words, "Where two or three are gathered in my name, I am there among them" (Matt 18:20); then in the service of the presider, in the word of God that is proclaimed, and only at the end of this process, this celebration, is he also present in an abiding manner in the Eucharist. All these modes of presence are real and may not be set in contrast to one another.

This dynamic conception of liturgy ruptures the medieval restriction of the validity of the sacraments to the minimum of matter and form and regains a dialogical view of the liturgy. It belongs to this dialogue between God and humanity that God addresses the people, so that in every liturgical celebration there is a proclamation of the Word of God, to which the community can then respond with praise, thanksgiving, and petition. The liturgical celebration of the sacraments can therefore no longer be so understood as if it were sufficient to bring about an action of God by means of a specific act and an accompanying formula; in the past, such a view may quite often have bordered on a magical misconception.

In the old rite of the Mass, the celebrant turned toward the altar, so that in a certain sense the celebration was directed toward the tabernacle. The priest brought the community behind him to a faith-consciousness that was concentrated primarily on the Blessed Sacrament. But the initial moment of Christ's presence is the Church assembled for prayer, the community gathered around the table of the Word and the table

[29] In: *Documents on the Liturgy 1963–1979. Conciliar, Papal, Curial Texts.* ICEL (Collegeville: The Liturgical Press, 1982) 471.

of the Eucharist, in which the disclosure of the mystery of his presence unfolds. A symbolic expression of this is celebration *versus populum*: the mystery unfolds in the midst of the assembly.

The new conception of liturgy thus involves a dynamic process of celebration that is realized first in the participants, then in the Word descending from God to God's community. If the Eucharistic presence is mentioned last, this implies no detraction from our understanding of the Eucharist; what is at issue is an acknowledgment, fundamentally new in contrast to previous conceptions, that all the modes of Christ's presence are real in the sense of actual presence: the event is made sacramentally present now. But what is crucial in the event is the Lord's turning, in person, to his community; for even his presence in the Eucharistic gifts is not something static, a presence in space, but rather a personal presence.

V. The Church's Worship as Celebration of the Concrete Community

There is no such thing as "the" worship of "the" Church, as the liturgical books of the Roman Church might suggest by the use of titles like *Missale Romanum* or *Rituale Romanum*. Liturgical celebration, as the action of an assembly of Christians, is always a partial Church action, because it can never involve more than a part of the whole Church. But because it is a Church action, it is also always the whole Church that is acting; it is the event that makes Jesus' saving actions present. It is evident that a worship service can never be anything but the worship of a concrete community, for—as Vatican II says in one of the few places where individual congregations are described in ecclesiological terms the

> Church of Christ is truly present in all legitimate local congregations of the faithful which, united with their pastors, are themselves called churches in the New Testament. For in their own locality these are the new people called by God, in the Holy Spirit and in much fullness (cf. 1 Thess 1:5) the new people called by God. In them the faithful are gathered together by the preaching of the gospel of Christ, and the mystery of the Lord's Supper is celebrated. . . . In any com-

munity existing around an altar, under the sacred ministry of the bishop, there is manifested a symbol of that charity and "unity of the Mystical Body, without which there can be no salvation." In these communities, even though frequently small and poor, or living far from any other, Christ is present. By virtue of Him the one, holy, catholic, and apostolic Church gathers together.[30]

On this basis we can speak of a Eucharistic ecclesiology, for when the Church, as the concrete, assembled community "celebrates the Eucharist, it realizes 'what it is,' the body of Christ," (1 Cor 10:17), as correctly stated in a 1982 consensus document of the Commission for Theological Dialogue between the Roman Catholic and Orthodox Churches, signed by Cardinal Ratzinger.[31] According to this, the Church in one place, the community assembly is

> fully such when it is the Eucharistic synaxis. When the local church celebrates the Eucharist, the event which took place "once and for all" is made present and manifested. In the local church, then, there is neither male nor female, slave nor free, Jew nor Greek. A new unity is communicated which overcomes divisions and restores communion in the one body of Christ. This unity transcends psychological, racial, socio-political or cultural unity. It is the "communion of the Holy Spirit". . . .[32]

Church is thus constituted by the individual communities that celebrate the Eucharist and are joined with one another by the Eucharist. Because such a description of the Church is structured "from the bottom up" and sees Church wherever a community celebrates the liturgy, in this document the office of the Pope is not required for a description of the Church. On the other hand, the service of the bishop, who is properly the presider at the Eucharist, is emphasized. Literally, it says:

> The eucharistic unity of the local church implies communion between him who presides and the people to whom he

---

[30] *LG* 26.

[31] "The Church, the Eucharist and the Trinity," *Origins* 12 (1982/83) 157–60, at I, 4b, 158.

[32] *Ibid.*, II, 1.

> delivers the word of salvation and the eucharistic gifts. Further, the minister is also the one who "receives" from his church, . . . the word he transmits. . . .[33]

The service of the bishop is thus seen as bound up with the Eucharistic celebration of his local Church. And perhaps more clearly than in the Constitution on the Liturgy, the communion between him and the congregation is described as follows:

> The bishop presides at the offering which is that of his entire community. By consecrating the gifts . . . the community offers, he celebrates not only for it [the community], nor only with it and in it, but through it,

for the "union of the community with [Christ] is . . . not primordially of the juridical order."

Thus this document can also describe the ideal of the ancient tradition, because in it

> the bishop elected by the people—who guarantee his apostolic faith, in conformity with what the local church confesses—receives the ministerial grace of Christ by the Spirit in the prayer of the assembly and by the laying on of hands of the neighboring bishops, witnesses of the faith of their own churches.[34]

In such a sacramental ecclesiological conception, proceeding from the Eucharist-celebrating community, the pope need not be mentioned separately, unless as bishop of Rome and therefore as presider in his local Church, for this Church community "is expressed traditionally through conciliar praxis."[35]

Incidentally, John Paul II's 1980 document "On the Mystery and Veneration of the Most Holy Eucharist" is quite similar. Walter Kasper writes that what emerges from this document is

> on the whole a sacramental, indeed a eucharistic conception of the Church, . . . corresponding entirely to the view of

[33] *Ibid.*, II, 3.
[34] *Ibid.*, II, 4.
[35] *Ibid.*, III, 4.

the church fathers. . . . The Eastern Church has preserved this point of view vividly until the present. The West [however] developed a more individualistic and juridical view, especially in the second millennium. . . . One need not be a prophet to say that such a eucharistic conception of the Church has far-reaching consequences for ecumenism. . . .[36]

A brief glance at the development of the relationship between Eucharist and community in the history of dogma can make it clear what an astonishing change this conception of the Eucharist implies for ecclesiology. Until the early Middle Ages, the language of faith meant by "real body" (*Corpus reale*) the Church, while "mystical body" (*Corpus mysticum, sacramentale*) meant the Eucharist. Since the Middle Ages the reverse is true: the mystical body is the Church; the real body, however, is the Eucharistic species.[37] Hence in the ancient Church the doctrine of the Eucharist and ecclesiology were closely related. The Eucharistic celebration was the basis of the unity of the congregation as well as its *communio* with other congregations in the *Una catholica*. But even before the end of the first millennium an individualizing of the conception of Eucharist had begun; Eucharistic doctrine and ecclesiology were separated, and the Church was no longer regarded as a *communio* of local Churches or individual congregations, but as a universal, socially-constituted entity. This latter was represented by offices, in a certain sense from top to bottom. The congregation no longer had any role to play, since the priest acted in the name of Christ and the Church. The Tridentine conflict with the Reformers did not sharpen the focus on the connection between community and Eucharist. On the contrary, it led to a more strongly juridical and social image of the Church, and after Trent the doctrine of the Eucharist, by its isolated treatment of the sacrificial character of the Eucharist obscured the ecclesial dimension. Only since Leo XIII (d. 1903), as a re-

[36] Text and commentary in: Walter Kasper, *Ein Leib und ein Geist werden in Christus. Schreiben über die Eucharistie Papst Johannes Pauls II* (Freiburg, 1980) 80–81.

[37] Cf. Henri de Lubac, *Corpus mysticum. Eucharistie und Kirche im Mittelalter* (Einsiedeln, 1969).

sult of the liturgical movement and Vatican II, has an understanding of the essential connection between Church and Eucharist emerged again. Especially in the constitutions on liturgy and on the Church, as well as in the Decree on the Service and Life of Priests, there are elements of a Eucharistic ecclesiology, although they stand isolated alongside other elements belonging to a universal ecclesiology.

Still, we may speak of a fundamentally new definition of this relationship by Vatican II. For the first time in the history of magisterial documents since the Middle Ages, the congregation is mentioned as an independent theological entity. At the same time, the community of the faithful is regarded as an active subject. We see the triumph of the idea that it is no longer the priest alone, but the community as a whole that is to be regarded as subject and agent of the liturgical action, because all believers share in the priesthood of Christ: "the Christian people as 'a chosen race, a royal priesthood, a holy nation, a purchased people' (1 Pet 2:9; cf. 2:4-5)" participate in the liturgy as "their right and duty by reason of their baptism."[38] This statement represents a "Copernican shift."[39]

This is the decisive step beyond Trent: the faithful celebrate the liturgy together with the presider. The common priesthood of believers who have been incorporated into the Church through baptism, confirmation, and first Eucharist is described as a sacerdotal priesthood, distinct from the presbyteral priesthood of the one who presides over the community. Theodor Schneider, dogmatic theologian from Mainz, correctly writes: "When we consider all that, we must certainly say that the concept of 'priest' . . . is not especially appropriate to describe the specific function of office in the Church."[40]

Schneider also sees in Vatican II the recovery of the conception of the early Church as *expressed* in the *symbolum*, the Credo:

> What constitutes the very core of the Church, according to the conception of the Apostles' Creed, is thus not primarily

[38] SC 14. Cf., *inter alia*, SC 48.

[39] According to Lengeling (see n. 19 above) 15.

[40] Theodor Schneider, *Zeichen der Nähe Gottes. Grundriß der Sakramententheologie* (Mainz, 1979) 246–47.

to be seen from the perspective of its offices or its organization, but from its liturgy. . . . The eucharistic assembly is the "constructive point" of the ancient Church's ecclesiology. The members of this community . . . are those who are joined in *communio* by the food from the one table.[41]

VI. The Identity of the Community and Its Worship

Far-reaching changes have occurred in the ecclesiology of the last decades. Following Adolf Exeler, the Münster pastoral theologian who died in 1983, we can distinguish on a broad scale "three types of ecclesiology: christocentric, theocentric, and pneumatological."[42] Before the Council the Church was primarily described, in the framework of a Christocentric ecclesiology, as the Body of Christ, and the Church was so thoroughly identified with Christ that its continual need for reform faded into the background—for in those circumstances, who could dare to criticize the Church, and thus be critical of Christ? In a theocentric ecclesiology like that emphasized at Vatican II, the Church is described as the people of God, so that not only the connection, but also the difference between Christ and the Church was emphasized, and with it the Church's constant need for reform. From this point on, an "appropriate criticism of the Church can even be a sign of love for the Church: a sign of the suffering that results when the Church is not what it could and should be."[43] Within a pneumatological ecclesiology the Church is understood as a movement enlivened by the Holy Spirit; this places less emphasis on the institutional aspects, and more on community in faith, hope, and love, the spirit of renewal that comes from the Spirit, and the gifts that each one receives from the Spirit for the upbuilding of the whole.

[41] *Idem*, "Die dogmatische Begründung der Ekklesiologie nach dem Zweiten Vatikanischen Konzil dargestellt am Beispiel der Rede von der Kirche als dem Sakrament des Heils für die Welt," in: Heinz Althaus, ed., *Kirche, Ursprung und Gegenwart* (Freiburg, 1984) 79–118, at 108.

[42] Adolf Exeler, "Gemeinde aus Männern und Frauen—ein Ensemble von Charismen," in: Franz Georg Friemel, ed., *Frauen in unserer Kirche* (Leipzig, n. d.) 236.

[43] *Ibid.*, 237.

This obviously has consequences for our understanding of the liturgy. If the Church is a living community of many Spirit-enlivened congregations, liturgy is not in the first place a matter of order and law; instead, the congregation is primary, and individual congregations should participate in giving form to the service of worship. Our understanding of Church and congregation therefore determines the celebration and form of the liturgy, and vice versa.

Karl Lehmann sees the construction of identity on the part of individual congregations in terms of the identity of their goals, which arise from the fundamental theological functions of the Church: "Ultimately, there are three central tasks of Church and congregation: testifying to the Gospel through the word, divine praise, and the love of brothers and sisters expressed in service." These three basic functions "are most deeply concentrated in the congregation's celebration of the Eucharist. Here the lordship of Jesus Christ is publicly acknowledged; here the congregation joins in praise and thanksgiving; from it Christians, in the memorial of the Lord's death and resurrection, derive the inexhaustible strength needed for surrendering themselves to the service of love. A Eucharistic celebration that does not extend itself as *diakonia* is not truly deserving of the name."[44]

When the congregation is described as the agent of the liturgy and the subject of the celebration, the particular conditions in each celebrating congregation must be taken into consideration. The preparation of liturgical books for different groups within the Church is an important step in that direction. In fact, we no longer have a Roman liturgy, but instead a Roman-German liturgy, since the German liturgical books are not simply translations of the normative Latin books. Still, we cannot yet speak of a true inculturation of the Christian liturgy in the German-speaking world, because the Missal, for example, is in its style and textual tradition a witness to the Franco-Roman liturgy as it had developed up to the end of the first millennium; it is a book of old texts that can scarcely respond to the faith-demands of our contemporary congrega-

[44] Karl Lehmann, "Gemeinde," *Christlicher Glaube in moderner Gesellschaft* 29 (Freiburg, 1982) 25 and 31–32.

tions. There is a wide discrepancy between the congregation assumed by our revised liturgical texts and the congregation that is really assembled.

If the congregation finds its identity in the liturgy and is supposed to express that identity in the liturgy, it needs an appropriate sphere of freedom in which it can develop. At the same time, it is indispensable that the liturgy correspond to Jesus' founding intention. There must also be assurance of continuity with the Church's tradition because what we celebrate today is essentially the same as what we celebrated yesterday, and what we celebrate here is the same as what happens in other congregations. In addition, this restriction protects the liturgy from private control and individual whim. Nevertheless, the congregation assembled for a specific reason must celebrate a liturgy appropriate to the situation. Attention must be paid to the reason for the celebration, the space in which it occurs, the ability of those assembled to comprehend what is happening, and their numbers, to mention only a few factors.

The indeterminate variety of situations demands a variety of possibilities. In the field of tension between obligation and freedom, the rule should be: as much regulation as necessary, and as much freedom as possible.[45] There is no once-and-for-all solution to this problem; each congregation must continually struggle to find the right way.

We could note, somewhat ironically, that every congregation celebrates the worship suitable for that community of believers. In fact, there are often substantial differences from congregation to congregation, and one can observe, from the form and progress of a worship service, how things are in this congregation and how it truly understands itself. The nonverbal signs cannot deceive. The very arrangement of the liturgical space, but especially the actions of those assembled, particularly the one presiding, clearly indicate whether this is a liturgy from above or from below.

At the same time, there is a mutual relationship between

---

[45] On this point, cf. the chapter entitled "Das Spannungfeld zwischen Ordnung und Freiheit, zwischen Einheit und Vielfalt im Gottesdienst der Kirche," in: Philipp Harnoncourt, *Gesamtkirchliche und teilkirchliche Liturgie. Untersuchungen zur praktischen Theologie* 3 (Freiburg, 1974) 50–59.

living community worship celebration and social commitment. As Karl Lehmann has written, "only in a zone of genuine brotherhood and sisterhood and of lived *diakonia* can the Eucharistic celebration be a full and undistorted sign of peace. Otherwise, it is difficult to distinguish it, theologically and practically, from sacramentalism."[46]

How different the worship service may appear from congregation to congregation, if it is to be the sign of each congregation's identity, Herbert Vorgrimler describes in this way:

> Liturgy was updated by the liturgical reform . . . in such a way that it was stripped of certain superfluous embellishments and assumed a form in which it can at least be understood by the "people." This reform could not and did not wish to cause this liturgy to cease being the liturgy of a hierarchy and instead to make it the business of the whole "people." I think it would be wrong to make continual efforts at reform in the direction of a well-intended popularization. On the contrary: the official liturgy should always be the most dignified witness to a rich ecclesial tradition. Alongside it, however, the people should be permitted to produce their own liturgies, out of their own spontaneity and creativity. . . . The hierarchy has achieved its own rights and its own liturgy. It is time to ask about the rights and the liturgy of the "people."[47]

Even if one thinks, as I do, that liturgical reform exists in the context of far-reaching shifts in theological emphasis, especially in the area of our understanding of Church and congregation, and that what is at issue is more than a "well-intended popularization," we should not ignore the fact that the opportunities involved have in a variety of ways not been exploited.

VII. Liturgical Reform and Church Reform

If I may, in conclusion, say a few words about those unexploited opportunities, I wish to emphasize that I am not con-

---

[46] "Gemeinde" (see n. 44 above) 33.

[47] Herbert Vorgrimler, "Liturgie als Thema der Dogmatik," in: Klemens Richter, ed., *Liturgie—ein vergessenes Thema der Theologie?* QD 107 (Freiburg, 2d ed. 1987) 125–27.

cerned here with questions of the concrete structuring of liturgies. A lot is at sixes and sevens in that area and a good deal of what we see in our congregations has little to do with what the reform had in mind. A statement of the German bishops applies here: they say that there appears to be "a deficiency in liturgical education among many priests and lay people, church musicians and religion teachers, professors and students of theology that is often hard to believe."[48] But surely the bishops' positive evaluation of the reform is also correct: here they say that there is a growth in awareness that the liturgy is celebrated not only by the priest, but by all those assembled, and that, as a result, there is an increasing perception "that those celebrating together belong to one another and together bear responsibility for each other and for the world."[49]

But if liturgical reform is not part of a general reform of the Church—including a reform of preaching and the theology that underlies it, as well as of the forms of Church organization—it will ultimately remain only a cosmetic treatment of the Church's image. In the German Church at the end of the second millennium we are faced with a contradictory pastoral situation. There are still a great many active congregations of the popular, national Church throughout the country, but at least in the major cities these structures have generally collapsed. We live in a totally secularized world in which our liturgy must appear to many as an anomaly of cultural behavior: to adopt a phrase of Joachim Wanke, the bishop of Erfurt, we seem like people who are trying to sell sunglasses to cave dwellers.[50] We have to develop forms of Christianity that are different from those we are used to. We will have to come to the point of appealing to individuals, drawing them into active communities of brotherhood and sisterhood, and living and praying with them. If the liturgy were the center of this kind of far more comprehensive way of life it could unfold its full dynamism. But if the liturgy is nothing more in the life

---

[48] "Der liturgische Dienst," Paper no. 8 in the German Bishops' Conference press kit for the papal visit of November 1980.

[49] "Zwanzig Jahre Liturgiekonstitution," *Gottesdienst* 17 (1983) 159.

[50] Cf. Klemens Richter, "Liturgie in säkularisierter Gesellschaft?" *Diakonia* 21 (1990) 21–29.

of individuals than a ritual carried out every Sunday, it will dry up and blow away.

A rethinking along these lines has not yet happened in this country. As an example, let me point to the failure to exploit the opportunities offered by the adult catechumenate. In the United States this is considered one of the most important results of the Council. Many congregations attempt to appeal to people outside, to draw them into active community and to accompany them on their way to membership in the Church. In this country, on the other hand, the liturgical book for the "Celebration of the Reception of Adults into the Church" is completely unknown in many places. To non-Christians the Church must appear as a building without doors; something you can only be born into. And so we also neglect the opportunity for a congregation to go with others on the journey of faith that the catechumenate opens to them.

Another neglected opportunity in light of our secularized world consists in our failure to inculturate our liturgy, particularly its language.[51] The liturgical books presuppose a congregation whose faith is secure and who participate in worship every day, if possible.

> Christians living in an environment marked by atheism . . . who struggle to achieve a minimum of faith so that they may continue to see themselves as Christians, who are forced by continually new questions posed by the circumstances of life and the conditions of the time into a kind of permanent catechumenate, and who, because their faith is weakened and in danger, have honest difficulties in producing even a minimum of response in faith, which is called prayer— such people must conclude with incredible logic that such a liturgy is something for the perfect, but not for Christians who have to live, after all, and probably by God's all-powerful providence as well, in these confusing times. And because the . . . Christians in such a situation are the nor-

[51] On this, cf. the fundamental observations of Hans Bernhard Meyer, "Zur Frage der Inkulturation der Liturgie," *ZKTh* 105 (1983) 1–31; *idem,* "Liturgie in lebenden Sprachen," in: Martin Klöckener and Winfried Glade, eds., *Die Feier der Sakramente in der Gemeinde. FS Heinrich Rennings* (Kevelaer, 1986) 331–45.

mal phenomena in our latitudes nowadays, this means precisely what the Council *cannot* have intended.[52]

This liturgy appears to have little to do with the lives of those who may well be the majority of Christians. If, for example, the meaning of the formulae in our Eucharistic prayers becomes clear even to students of theology only after several hours of lectures, how much more is this true of other believers?

The route from a Eurocentric to a pluriform world Church will be determined, among other things, by the liturgy. The Roman Church has now accepted about four hundred liturgical languages. Celebrating faith in one's own language and culture leads inevitably to one's own rituals, for which that in Zaire may serve as an example. It is evident from the history of the Church and the liturgy that regional liturgies have always led to the development of independent regional Churches. I do not doubt that, precisely as a result of liturgical developments, in the long run the Roman patriarchy will be able to preserve unity only in diversity, through the development of a number of sister Churches. For a long time now, this also has remained an unexploited opportunity, and it, too, is conditioned by the connection between our understanding of Church and of liturgy.

There can be no doubt that the liturgy is inevitably drawn into the process of change that the Church must endure in order to be faithful to its mission. It seems a matter of course that this process involves danger and anxiety. But the difficulties connected with it cannot be solved by talking about a crisis in the liturgy; nothing will do but to take hold, in faith, on the work that has been entrusted to the Church. Part of this is that we must not choose what appears the easiest way and simply cling to what has been received from the past. The communion of believers must, like Abraham, listen to God's call: "Go from your country and your kindred . . . to the land that I will show you" (Gen 12:1). This pilgrimage is a risk, but one we can dare to take, secure and trusting in the Lord whom

---

[52] Angelus A. Häußling, "Ist die Reform der Stundenliturgie beendet odor noch auf dem Weg?" in: *Lebt unser Gottesdienst?* (see n. 21 above) 234.

we know to be present in our midst when we celebrate the liturgy.[53]

The liturgical reform that sees the community as the agent of liturgical action is unthinkable without a corresponding reform of Church and congregational structures. Many of the foot-dragging orders "from the top" that are opposed to the principle of *liturgia semper reformanda* may be connected with the fact that we are beginning to recognize the consequences that a renewed liturgy will have for our understanding of Church and community. Only where steps are taken on the road from a community that is cared for to one that cares for itself, only where we are serious about a theological acknowledgment of a Eucharistic ecclesiology, according to which the whole Church is built up by the individual congregations celebrating the Eucharist, only where an *ecclesia semper reformanda* is not only proclaimed, but lived—only there will that be effected which the Council in the very first sentence of the Constitution on the Liturgy set as its goal: "to intensify the daily growth of Catholics in Christian living; to make more responsive to the requirements of our times those Church observances which are open to adaptation; to nurture whatever can contribute to the unity of all those who believe in Christ. . . ."[54] Then liturgical reform can achieve its true meaning, namely, by becoming the center of a constant reform of Church and community. Even now, twenty-five years after the Council, it is by no means certain that this goal will be fully attained.

[53] Cf. Heinrich Rennings, "Aus Treue" (n. 27 above) 160–61.
[54] *SC* 1.

The Authors

Angelus A. Häussling, O.S.B., is a monk of the Abbey of Maria Laach and professor of liturgy at the School of Philosophy and Theology of Benediktbeuern, Germany.

Philipp Harnoncourt is professor of liturgy at the University of Graz, Austria.

Klemens Richter is professor of liturgy at the University of Münster, Germany.

Philipp Schäfer is professor of dogmatic theology and the history of doctrine at the University of Passau, Germany.

Richard Schaeffler is professor emeritus of philosophical theology in the Catholic Theological Faculty of the University of the Ruhr, Bochum, Germany.

Clemens Thoma, S.V.D., is professor of biblical studies and Judaism and director of the Institute for Jewish-Christian Studies in the Faculty of Theology at the University of Lucerne, Switzerland.